Leadership

Ultimate Guide to Beeing A Successful and Charismatic Leader

(Learn Team Building and Employee Management Skills At Workplace)

Shawn Verner

Published By **Regina Loviusher**

Shawn Verner

All Rights Reserved

Leadership: Ultimate Guide to Beeing A Successful and Charismatic Leader (Learn Team Building and Employee Management Skills At Workplace)

ISBN 978-1-77485-624-6

No part of this guidebook shall be reproduced in any form without permission in writing from the publisher except in the case of brief quotations embodied in critical articles or reviews.

Legal & Disclaimer

The information contained in this ebook is not designed to replace or take the place of any form of medicine or professional medical advice. The information in this ebook has been provided for educational & entertainment purposes only.

The information contained in this book has been compiled from sources deemed reliable, and it is accurate to the best of the Author's knowledge; however, the Author cannot guarantee its accuracy and validity and cannot be held liable for any errors or omissions. Changes are periodically made to this book. You must consult your doctor or get professional medical advice before using any of the suggested remedies, techniques, or information in this book.

Upon using the information contained in this book, you agree to hold harmless the Author from and against any damages, costs, and expenses, including any legal fees potentially resulting from the application of any of the information provided by this guide. This disclaimer applies to any damages or injury caused by the use and application, whether directly or indirectly, of any advice or information presented, whether for breach of contract, tort, negligence, personal injury, criminal intent, or under any other cause of action.

You agree to accept all risks of using the information presented inside this book. You need to consult a professional medical practitioner in order to ensure you are both able and healthy enough to participate in this program.

Table of Contents

Chapter 1: Making First Impressions 1

Chapter 2: Team Member 16

Chapter 3: Contexts/Your Position, Making The Most Of It 21

Chapter 4: Actualization 39

Chapter 5: The Performance Equation ... 59

Chapter 6: Individual Decision Making ... 72

Chapter 7: The Skills Of A Leader 80

Chapter 8: Authority Eats First. Leaders Eat Last 98

Chapter 9: The Ability To Decide On Tough Issues 109

Chapter 10: Communicator 114

Chapter 11: A Leaders Communication 123

Chapter 12: Established Leadership Styles
.... 141

Chapter 13: Taking Risks 148

Chapter 14: Task-Oriented Leadership. 163

Chapter 15: Continue To Expand Your Skills
.... 174

Conclusion 182

Chapter 1: Making First Impressions

Here's your guide to making great first impressions. This will help you grow your business and personal wealth. You can influence nearly 85 percent your business success by how you interact with people in the first 30 second of meeting them. It only takes a split second for someone to decide whether or not they like you. It doesn't sound scary! It is. Just imagine. These initial 30 seconds will make or break your career. You have put in thousands of hours learning and doing hardwork to build your career.

Why are First Impressions Important?

Still not worried? You might be able to recall the last time you met someone new. Perhaps it was a bank employee, a possible connection to a network, or the friend of a friend who works with a major brand. It could be your neighbor's friend, who is a mother to a gorgeous child or two about your age. What did these encounters look and feel like? What did they say? How did it look? What did you wear?

Your success will depend on how you behave and present yourself to others. The first impression is key to opening many doors, pointing out shortcuts, as well as helping you make lasting connections. How do they do it? How can people remember you so they want to talk with you in under a minute? Lucky for us, we have the answer.

Before we start talking about strategies to make an impression and how to do it, let's talk briefly about why this is so difficult. Your fight-or flee response triggers when you're about meeting someone new. Your unconscious brain evaluates your feelings about the person you are going to be with and is particularly attentive to anything that might be threatening. You can see that first encounters are a dynamic with two or more people. Immediately, they decide whether the new person is safe to be around. Your unconscious mind is able to detect the body language, general appearance, and other particularities of the other person and draw conclusions. Your peers and family members will also be able to see the difference. A great way to make an impression is to use more "green flags," rather than "red flags." This means being safe and avoiding unintentional danger signals.

How to radiate genuine positivity and make a great first impression

Positive attitudes allow you to be your best through your thoughts and actions. To be positive, it must come from within and not just be imposed. It is important to keep working on your perception of the world in order to keep a positive, optimistic perspective and to acknowledge the realities. A rule of thumb is that people tend to prefer positive people. But if your job as a grief consultant is to make people happy, then you shouldn't act stoic and upbeat. When you're dealing with someone in this situation, it is important to have empathy. However, you must also be positive about how you communicate and interact with them. Talking to people in a social setting such as a company or party is a great way to be confident and upbeat. What do you do if it's not appropriate? Then you need to adapt to make it better.

Toxic positivity on the other side is present in people that we perceive as disingenuous. These people claim false success stories and boast about the abilities of others. It's easy for people to notice that their motives are self-involved. They can only fool those who have the ability to be emotionally and psychologically vulnerable. But even that is temporary. If you are talking about positivity, remember that it means a genuine, positive attitude and mannerisms designed to make everyone around you feel better than they ever felt before they met. This may be done with humor at times or through words of support and consolation.

7 Steps for Radiating Positiveness:

1. Keep the moment.

Focus on the situation and the people in it to display this quality. Keep your cool, and don't let anyone take it away. It is difficult to keep yourself safe from those who we might call "toxic". Do not react to any other person's provocative or toxic behavior if you find yourself in a situation. If your reaction isn't helping or bringing about any improvement, you shouldn't respond.

2. Modify your appearance.

Our first impressions make all the difference, whether we like to admit it or not. You may be judged by how you come across in the first few minutes whether you are offered a job promotion, a date or a client. Everyone has been taught that it is better not to be concerned about what people think of us. But it is essential to be aware of how the first few seconds can influence how others view you. This could include your facial expressions or body language as well as your mannerisms. People judge your personality based upon what they see. What about making a great first impression by changing your appearance? There are a few things you can try to show your authenticity, be genuine, and respect others.

Demonstrate respect How can you expect others to respect you? To show respect, you must first be considerate of the time and feelings of others. Being punctual is key. It is important to be on time and punctual when meeting new people. It's possible to make a bad first impression by arriving late at your first appointment.

Take care of your own personal image. Consider how you present yourself to the occasion. Your outfit should be appropriate to the occasion. It should reflect you and your unique personality. The outfit does not have to be luxurious. You don't have always to be elegant to make the right impression. A well-chosen outfit will leave a lasting impression. And what better way than to showcase your amazing style? But it is essential that you look professional at all times, whether you are at work and at networking events. Different occasions will require you to wear different clothes.

It wouldn't be the same outfit you wear to work that you wear to a wedding. There are many chic, timeless and classic outfits that work for many different occasions. The "little white dress" is an example of a uniform style that you can wear from work to the wedding. It's also versatile in terms of accessories and styling. The simple elegance of plain black pants, a blazer, and any neutral-colored shirt is suitable for most settings. Think about investing in some classic chic, timeless pieces you can wear every day.

Be authentic. Be authentic. To be charismatic, it is important to fit in. You want to fit in, but still be different. It is important to have connections with the group or an environment, regardless of whether they are working together to achieve a common goal or solving a problem. To be authentic, one must show respect and integrity. Respecting the integrity, and self-respect, of people you meet is an important part of being authentic. This will help build confidence and expand social networks.

3. Don't be afraid to smile.

People remember people who smile and are happy. Smiles are a sign of warmth and confidence. It will help others feel good. Be careful not to smile too artificially. It can look unnatural, creepy, and insecure and may give the wrong impression.

4. Don't be afraid to show your confidence

Confidence can be one of the most appealing qualities. It is more important than your resume. You can make others feel secure by showing confidence through your body language and eye contact. It is common to feel insecure around people. You can work with your anxiety or nervousness before you meet and take time to relax. If you want to look confident and relaxed when you meet someone for the very first time, it is important to plan ahead.

There is another way to handle this type of nervousness. It is to accept it and to be completely comfortable with it. People laugh about their awkwardness and social mishaps. This helps everyone feel more comfortable. There is nothing wrong in being shy. There's nothing wrong with being shy. But you should try to stop your shyness from preventing you from connecting and making friends.

5. Practice small talk.

Small talk can be used to answer seemingly mundane questions. Even though small talk sounds irrelevant, it isn't. Small talk is a way to learn more about ourselves and make connections. Every verbal exchange creates a dynamic of information sharing and receiving.

6. Increase your emotional intelligence

The best way to learn how to communicate emotion intelligence and make your first impressions is to do it. It might seem that your work results, talents and abilities speak for themselves. But the truth is much more complicated. People subconsciously draw much more conclusions that they would care to admit. It is essential that you have the ability to communicate your emotions and interpret them. This will help you make a good first impression. These skills help you communicate well, to resolve conflicts, negotiate and work together towards the same goal in every situation. People will view you as trustworthy and reliable when they see your sharp emotional intelligence.

But what is emotional Intelligence? It's the ability to perceive emotions and make decisions. It means being able to recognize the emotions and motives of others by looking beyond superficial behavior. To master these skills you must first learn to have emotional awareness. This means being able to perceive how you feel. You will also be able to recognize how your emotions impact your motivations, decisions and behavior. There are two ways to cultivate your emotional intelligence.

It is important to practice self-reflection. Self-reflection enables you to examine your thoughts and feelings, and then, critically, how those affect your actions. Before you arrive to your meeting take a few minutes to think about how you feel in these situations and what you think. This will help to match your attitude to the person who you are speaking to or to the situation you are in. Your mindset could become too inward-focused and cause you to lose touch with the situation.

Level your energy. How to adjust your energies to the situation and the person that you're talking to can help you communicate and connect with them. When you're proficient in emotional intelligence, you'll be able adapt your body language to the situation and your energy to it. How you conduct yourself in formal settings or at wedding parties will require different approaches.

You should be able to focus on the other person. Listening to what the other person has to say and being attentive will help you build rapport and leave an impression. This requires that you remove all distractions and put your phone away to maintain natural, steady eyecontact. In order to not appear bored or uninterested in another person's conversation, it is important that you don't interrupt them. It's possible to appear uninterested if you speak to another person and then think about the next thing that you want to say.

7. Concentrate on common interests.

Talking to someone who makes you feel comfortable is a great way to find common interests. This will make it easier for the other person to remember that you were related to them, especially if your topic was entertaining and interesting. Asking questions is a great way of finding common interests with another person. You should not come off as an interrogator. A shy person might be uncomfortable answering questions.

Master the Art and Science of Asking and Answering Question

When starting a conversation, it is common to ask some questions about the other person. In informal settings like meetings and job interviews, those at the top will open the conversation and pose questions. Those looking for work or money will be the ones answering. Keep your answers short and simple when answering common questions. What does this mean exactly?

Unless asked to do so, you shouldn't give one-word answers. Being shy can make it difficult to answer questions like "Where is your family from?" or "What do they do?". Instead, try to give more details about yourself. You can also comment on things that you like or appreciate about your place and your work. Also, you can tell your story about how you got involved in the current job.

Apart from the common questions, it is common to be asked about your work and career during interviews or networking events. Here are some specific questions to be answered during job interviews.

"Why are you the right person?" The interviewer will ask you about your motivations, and how excited you are to be a part of the company. In this section, you should talk about your experience and skills and how they can benefit the organization.

Interviewers will want information about your motivations for changing jobs. They will also be curious about your work and employment records, and why you left the previous job. It's important to give clear, genuine answers. Otherwise you may leave a bad impression.

Interviews allow you to ask questions. This will allow you to get more information about the job they have posted. Asking questions regarding details is an act of initiative. It also shows that you are interested not only in a job but the whole company.

Ask about leadership and career progression. This question will depend on many factors, most importantly on the company's culture. If you find that the company values personal development and leadership, you might be able to talk about your goals and learn how the position matches your plans for personal growth. If you aren't convinced that this approach is appropriate for the job you are applying for, you might be interested in senior management or other team members. They can ask about their career paths and tell you how long they have been with the company.

Summary

This chapter taught you that first impressions can have a huge impact on your success. The key to making a great first impression is to:

* Be kind, considerate, and aware of the needs of those around you

* Display confidence with your appearance and posture.

Learn how to master casual conversation

* Talk about mutual-interest topics.

* Ask and answer open-ended, relevant questions that are both interesting, strategic and appropriate.

Now that you're confident in your first impression, let's learn how to exude real confidence. The next chapter will help you to create and maintain the rock-solid confidence required to be a true leader.

Chapter 2: Team Member

A potential team organizer must decide who to select based upon the task. Two perspectives can be used to view this. The functional view, in which it is more important that the person be able to perform the job well, is one way. It is possible to see the person's ability to collaborate and work with other people. This second perspective allows you to shift your focus from task capability. Ideal situation is when the person can have both. In the real world, you need to pick a team that is diverse but open enough for everyone to work together.

Each person is the result and accumulation of their experiences. You can tell if someone is goal-oriented by how they were raised, how they react to life's events, or if they get distracted by the challenges they face.

This can be done by having them undergo a psychological evaluation. Psychevals, as they're known, are a collection of simple questions that aim to uncover the true character of a person.

The answers to certain combinations of questions can be answered by people with a specific character. The personality of every person who answers the same question in different ways is not the same. It means that an individual who answers one set of questions the same way will also respond in the same fashion to a situation (understanding those questions). A person's character profile is established when all their different traits are considered.

From this point, it's possible determine if a person truly is a loner and if they are social butterflies. Additionally, one can assess whether the person can listen to criticism objectively and constructively. Once all the areas have been determined, the next step is to get a composite. Software applications even exist that can manage and choose the best-fit team.

Although automated selection is a success, there are many things that can be improved. This way of selecting a team member introduces bias. Each of us has a certain set assumptions based in our past experiences. This bias is built into the algorithm.

It doesn't matter how many people we can qualify and classify, if we only find ten, then we will not be able build the perfect group. As soon as the team is assembled, their personalities are flexible and they often behave outside of the norm.

It's not beneficial to invest too much time or resources in finding the perfect match.

But what is most important is to get everyone on the same page and make the goal the priority. The goal is what unites all of us.

This characteristic is vital. Human beings work in degrees. They are not always the same thing. They each have different issues, baggage, presumptions or biases. Each is exposed to it in varying levels. The person you choose to be your teammate is the one with all the issues but can still work together for the common objective.

This characteristic allows two types to rise to the top. The one is by design a leader. The other is a followinger and neither one of them are confused about that. Your bottom-tier selections are made up of people who can't see beyond their narrowed vision. They are not leaders because what is in their minds at that time would be what they're following. They don't serve as followers; whatever is the current issue, it will be what they focus on. The team can't function without them. The axiom "A chain is only as strong its weakest link" should be remembered when choosing a team.

A person brought into the team must be able and capable of focusing his attention away external attention grabers and on the task at-hand. This includes the ability to mobilize resources from within a team. It is important to remember that personal biases can only be secondary to achieving the goal.

This is a normal human tendency. A leader or organizer of a team must choose someone who will place the collective interest above all else.

But, it is important that the person has the ability to do the job. Even though a team player may be great, if a person doesn't have the technical ability necessary to complete the task then all else is meaningless. This is why all our discussions are centered on this factor.

Once the neutrality of motivations and the ability to focus on an objective are established, then it's time to motivate the person to be the best.

There are two types that are best for this motivation: people who are easily motivated, and people who aren't. It is much easier to motivate people for the cause when the team has the right people.

Once you have found someone who is technically compatible, doesn't get distracted by outside stimuli, and is capable of being motivated, then you can find a member of the group that has high chances of succeeding.

Chapter 3: Contexts/Your Position, Making The Most Of It

An entrepreneur is responsible in organizing various factors, including capital, labor, machinery, and other resources. The entrepreneur organizes these factors to make them more productive. The product passes through many channels and agencies before finally reaching its final destination. The business activities can be broken down into various functions and each function assigned to different individuals.

One person cannot achieve a common goal for a business. Many people must work together to make it successful. The organization provides a framework for individuals to come together and delegate their roles and responsibilities. The management is responsible of combining diverse business activities in order to reach predetermined goals.

The current business system is very complex. The business system must function smoothly in order to maintain its position in the business community. Multiple jobs must be done by different people who are qualified. The functions of all these authorities require that they be divided into distinct groups. You can assign authority or responsibilities based on your function.

Concepts of Organization

There are 2 types of organizational concepts:

Static Concept

This defines an organization as either a structure, or a network of entities that are made up specific relationships. The static organization is simply a group of people that come together and form formal relationships in order to reach a common goal. It is more interested in the positions than it is the individuals.

Dynamic Concept

This concept explains that an organization is an ongoing and continuous process. A process by which people, work, processes, and systems are organized is called an organization. It is the process of determining which activities are necessary to achieve a given goal. It also involves the organization of these activities into teams so they can all be assigned. This concept considers that the organization is an open and adaptive system. It is not a closed-off system, unlike the static idea. Individuals are key to a dynamic idea.

Management

Management is the art and science that brings people together to attain the same goal. This requires coordination and integration with all resources. Management refers to all tasks and activities that are done in order to achieve a particular goal. These activities include planning for, controlling, organizing, and leading.

Management involves making decisions, planning, leading and organizing people, as well as motivating and controlling them. Management includes planning and controlling informational and physical resources within an organization in order to make it reach the top in a cost-effective and efficient manner.

Management can also be understood in a broad sense as:

Management is an Economic Factor

I asked an economist to explain that management is a major factor in the production process. Management's growth can be directly attributed to increasing industrialization. Managerial staff are charged with deciding whether profitability and productivity will be achieved. Because of its direct responsibility for rapid development, executive training is even more essential in these firms.

Management is a System of Authority

Managers see management as a system for authority. Management was created in ancient times as an autoritarian philosophy. It became more paternalistic over time. After the paternalistic approach, it developed into constitutional management. In this model, consistent policies are the most important concerns. It has become more democratic, participative and participatory.

Modern management is a hybrid of the above four approaches.

Management is a Class & Status System

Sociologists often refers to management as a "class-and-status" system. Modern society is becoming more complex. Because of this, managers should be extremely educated and well-informed. A person who wishes to be a leader must be extremely educated and have a lot to learn. Your education is more important that your political or familial connections. Some scholars claim that this is the 'Managerial Revolution.

Management can be very individualistic. People may have different views. However, management's ultimate aim is to accomplish a goal in an efficient yet effective manner.

Management: A Key Feature

Management is the process and result of reaching and achieving goals in a timely and efficient manner. Each aspect of management is different. Let's take a look at the different qualities of this process.

Management and Group Efforts

Management is often associated w/group efforts. Although people can manage their own affairs independently, managing in groups is easier. Every organization needs groups to achieve its goals. It has been shown that goal achievement is easier when groups are created.

Management and Purposefulness

Management doesn't exist without a purpose. Management is all about the achievement and promotion of goals. A measure of how successful management is can be used to determine the success or failure of its employees. Effective management is the best way to achieve your goals.

Management and the Efforts Others

Management can often be described as accomplishing tasks with the help and support of others. Management is essential for an organization to survive. An organization cannot survive without its managers. All their work must be integrated in the work of the manager.

Management and Goal-orientedness

Management is about achieving a goal. Management is about achieving a goal. These managers know where to start and how they can keep it moving. Managers tend to be highly goal-oriented. They also know how to get their employees to follow their lead.

Management is essential

Management is essential. It can't be replaced. Many people thought that computers would make managers obsolete. However it was quickly proven that computers are able to help but not replace managers. Computers can broaden the perspective of managers and enhance their insight. They help managers make quick decisions. The computer allows managers the ability to do analysis that is beyond normal human abilities. In reality, however, the computer is unable to work on its own nor pass any judgment. Even virtual reality and artificial intelligent cannot replace managers. Because the manager can use his imagination and provide judgement, he or she will remain relevant.

Management is an intangible

Management is sometimes referred to as an invisible force. Its presence is felt in the efforts and motivation shown by employees. It is also visible in the efficiency and discipline of the team.

Management and Better Life

Managers can be responsible for many things. Managers can help improve work environments and inspire group members to perform at their best. He or She can instill a sense o hope in the members of the group.

Group

Man is social and loves to live with others. The group could be a society (club, family), college, institute or college, as well as any other social organization. This instinct is also seen in animals like leopards. Leaders are individuals who take charge of groups. Leaders are expected to demonstrate commitment, vision, drive and determination to realize the group's purpose. It is basically the management of a group. The leader should be able motivate and inspire members of the group. The leader should also demonstrate flexibility and adaptability.

Project Management Management by Group Leadership

A project is any task that a group undertakes. It could be software design, building a structure, managing social networks, or any other task. A plan is crucial in the initial phases. A plan should include goals, members, and motivation, as well as budget details.

Teamwork

Team leaders should be able lead members of the group effectively. All members of the team need to have an environment conducive for effective and efficient work. This is a list containing the things that every member of the team needs.

- All members are given equal opportunities for growth.

A safe place to work. This includes physical, as well as mental safety.

Respect each member of the group. Respect is earned through respect.

- Any conflicts that arise within the group should be resolved in an amicable manner.

Regular meetings should occur to keep track of the group's progress. They should also be used to identify and resolve problems.

- When there is a failure, it should be properly discussed.

- Celebrate any success.

- Leaders should be open to receiving honest feedback from their members.

Once the feedback has been received, it must be analyzed. Corrective measures should also be taken.

Self-leadership

What is self-leadership and how can it be achieved?

Self-leadership may be defined as the ability or capability to inspire others and make a positive impact on your work and performance. It is connected to mastery as well as personal excellence. Self-leadership closely relates to selfconfidence, selfefficacy, as well as your self-beliefs. Self-leadership directly relates to your ability and confidence to accomplish goals or complete tasks. Self-leadership will allow you to be your best selves and help you create a personal brand. It forces you to compete with you, which can help your achieve both professional and personal goals.

It is vital to be a leader in this world.

It is highly competitive in today's world. It changes almost daily. It is important to be different and outstanding if your goal is to stand out in a crowd. It is important to communicate clearly, concisely, and boldly so that others can understand what you have to say.

The foundations you create will help you be a leader. The team will be responsible for the direction, commitment and alignment. True, leadership and self leadership are two different things. But they complement each others.

How to be a self-leader?

You will need to be passionate and dedicated in order to attain self-leadership. These are some tips that will help you become a self-leader.

Purpose and purpose in life

The leader who is self-aware must ask this question every day: "What purpose does my existence serve?" Without a purpose you will find yourself at the mercy your fate. It is important to have a clear plan and a sense you purpose. This helps you stay focused and can help you develop strategies that will help reach your goals.

Blind Spots

Blind spots are those aspects of your personality, which include feelings and values. These blind areas must be identified. This awareness requires courage as well as boldness. It involves receiving feedback from others. Often, this is from your subordinates. This will help to improve your self-awareness and ultimately make you more successful.

Building Character

Personal character includes both behavior and mental characteristics. This personal characteristic sets you apart. It displays moral potency, which is closely related to moral efficacy. Integrity is linked to character. Integrity refers only to those characteristics that are trustworthy and reliable. A leader should always be true to their promises and values. Respectability is possible when you are consistent with your beliefs. Reputation is important for effective leadership. It can even become your most valuable asset.

Integrity and Ethics

To become a selfless leader, you must be selfless. You should be ethical, and you should also possess integrity. Fair, honest, and varied are the best qualities. Ethics should be a priority and should not be left to the chance.

Family

Families are similar to many organizations, especially community groups. There are many families to choose from, including extended families, modern nuclear families and single parents. All these varieties are often seen in the modern day. These leadership principles are shared by nearly all these families. This principle can be applied to bring success and happiness to your family.

Importance leadership in families

There are many different ways leadership can benefit the family. Family should be supportive of each other's personal growth. A leader can encourage family members to grow in a holistic fashion. Family leaders who are good at helping family members grow in a holistic way aren't just concerned with their material needs, but also their emotional needs.

Balance

Leadership is necessary if you are to manage the many needs of the family. While one member of the family may have the upper hand at times due to injury or illness, others will need to be able to support the family.

Children are more important than children, and they should be treated as such. This is especially true if parents are involved.

A family's imbalance can also be caused by one adult ruling the family. For example, if the mother (the head) makes it difficult for her family to live a bizarre lifestyle of isolation and denial then the whole family will suffer. Children of the family suffer from this imbalance.

A Common Goal

Leadership in the family helps to establish a common goal. This ensures that the family is happy, healthy, & fulfilled. A family requires a vision, just like any other organisation. A family must have a goal or mission that all its members can agree to.

This mission focuses on the success and development of children.

Family leadership

In most families, the parent who is in charge of the leadership position is the one with the majority of the children. Sometimes, the leadership role can be shared equally by both parents. Other times, it can be held solely by one or both of the parents. It depends on the way each parent approaches leadership. It all depends upon the leader's handling of the responsibilities.

It is important to remember that families function just like other businesses. The rules of leadership can help a family leader achieve respect, success and authority. The leader of the family should possess the same leadership abilities as other leaders. These qualities include being open-minded, communicating well, fairness, integrity and commitment as well generosity.

CEO

A CEO (or Chief Executive Officer) is a leader with many facets. They must possess many different skills and knowledge.

Initially, companies would only hire those who had previous administration experience. Today, organizations are open to hiring leaders with different capabilities and allowing them to make the organization more competitive in the modern marketplace.

A leader isn't born. You can become a great leader by practicing and dedicating your time. It takes practice and dedication to become a great leader.

Inspiring people how to do things

Leaders need to be able inspire others. Leaders must be able and willing to communicate with others in order to motivate them to perform their tasks efficiently. CEOs, as well as other bosses, need to recognize that employees can be connected with others to achieve efficient work and a good work ethic. Honesty leads to honesty.

Rapidity

As stated above, the world continues to undergo rapid and continuous changes. Change is in every corner of the world. Rapid changes are taking place in almost all facets of the corporate world. There are technological, financial, social, economic, and societal shifts.

These changes all impact the corporate environment and create problems. These problems, which were once solved in the past few years, are back with a vengeance. Old solutions are no more effective. The leader should be able understand the principles of change and adapt to the times. He or She should be able and capable to lead his/her group towards change, adaptation, and growth.

Emotional Intelligence

The final chapter of this book discusses emotional intelligence as an idea.

Education won't make you a great teacher. Leaders have to be able do their jobs well. Leaders are permitted to make very few mistakes unlike other jobs. The essential skills required to be a successful leader include trustworthiness. Vision, acumen and high emotional intelligence. These skills only can be learned with hard work, practice, and dedication. Visionaries are great leaders who can motivate their team.

Chapter 4: Actualization

The most dangerous myth in leadership is that leaders are born. It is absurd. The contrary is true. Leaders are made and not born.

--Warren Bennis

Leadership does not emerge from nothing. You do not get it suddenly.

King and queens are born into leadership positions. But does their inheritance make them automatically leaders? No. Before they become great leaders, some will need to endure a lot of upheavals and training. Leaders are like gold being tested under fire. Some people are not born to be leaders, even though they receive the most sophisticated training.

Sometimes, a monarch is so gracious that people do not mind that his family was once a line of leaders who believed that God chose them.

Joseph II, the Austrian King, struggled with making the right choice between an authoritative figure and a compassionate leader. He had difficulties with controlling his state. He did so much for his people, like encouraging religious tolerance and abolishing a feudal system. These actions show that he cared more about the needs and wants of the people than the desires of the state.

Plato suggested having an philosopher-king. He believed that the leader should be skilled in reasoning and practice. Plato also believed that knowledge in philosophy would help a leader lean more towards being virtuous.

Leadership is about achieving your goals and becoming who you're meant to be.

Now, take a look at you and ask these questions:

Do I consider myself a leader or a follower in my work?

What are my short term and long term goals?

Do I want the title of leader? Why or pourquoi not?

What image do you see your actualized self looking like?

Why did your search for this book lead you to it?

Consider second what you could bring to the table.

What are your abilities and talents?

What weaknesses would you like to change?

What is self actualization?

It is the process that you reach your full potential. You drive is a key factor in your ability to get through this process. You won't be able to achieve the leader you deserve if you don't have this drive.

Leadership and Maslow's Hierarchy o Needs

Self-actualization, according to Maslow's hierarchy for needs, is the most important. It is the highest level of desire a person could strive for.

Why would you set your sights on something more? Being a leader is something you desire. A leader inspires. He realizes that he must push himself to achieve his goal, or at least try valiantly to help others do the same. How can leaders exist if everyone is content with just surviving at the bottom?

The leader can also be a straggler. He just has to learn how to be himself. Self-actualization is difficult.

Metaphorically, the world is full people who are standing at different rungs on the corporate ladder. Some could be described climbing the slippery edges Maslows' pyramid. What matters is that some are striving to rise in rank.

Sometimes, though, it can be challenging to rise in ranks. Donna wanted to self-actualize. Since her childhood, Donna felt the need and desire to improve her family's situation. Donna was unable to do much about the legacy of poverty that plagued her family through generations. It wasn't until she was offered a college fellowship that she started to believe there was hope. She was the youngest member of her family who graduated when she was 18. She believed that it was the end for all her troubles.

Donna was wrong. Her family relied on her even more. That is why she focused so much of her attention on getting more money. If her bosses offered additional development training, she was hesitant to accept it because she already had a job. Donna was forced to stay at Maslow's bottom because of her circumstance.

Now what if she was compared to Phillip? Phillip was also born to a poor family. However, Phillip lived almost entirely alone. His parents provided Phillip with the freedom to pursue whatever he desired. Phillip felt the need to provide for family members in some way. Phillip made the wise decision to provide his family a way of living. He started a small retail shop so that his parents could earn their income. Phillip was able then to achieve something better. Phillip was already secure in his family and felt loved. He was driven by his family's well-being and self-esteem. He only had to think about his career, and how he could achieve his goals.

In summary, each person has his or her own Maslow's path. It is wrong for us to judge others based on what they show. We cannot say, "Oh that person has no ambition at ALL." Sometimes, the circumstances grip us too tightly. The fact you found this book indicates that you are interested leadership. Leadership at its finest is about self fulfillment. Be the leader you wish to be.

Physiological and Medical Needs

It's enough for most people to feed their basic needs at Maslow's bottom. People who have physiological needs are happy to do what it takes to live a normal life. People stuck at this level will find it easier to change their loyalties.

Is it possible to be a leader when all you care about is your survival? You might be able to, but that would depend on what situation you are in. There is a simple setup that will save people from these physiological demands. This is how it probably began with hunting and gathering societies a long, long time ago.

A surprising discovery by anthropologists was that hunters or gatherers do not have permanent leaders. Leadership would be given to anyone who initiated a hunt or gathering session. Everyone was entitled to take the lead.

Security

As you progress up the ladder, you'll be thinking about your security. Your safety and that of your followers is a priority as a leader.

An employer, for example, must ensure that employees work in a safe and secure environment. It is more likely that they will feel inspired to work at their personal workspace if this quality is apparent. They know that someone cares about what they do. Safety leadership is now a concept all its own. People who show this knowledge are well-versed in the business. They use this knowledge to ensure that workers are safe.

You can go back in time to see how long it took for people to ensure the safety of their workers. Security is now synonymous with protection. In order to survive battles for example, you join a stronger group.

Some employees still advocate for improved safety in the workplace. Good leaders have listened to their concerns throughout this century.

Senses of belonging

How can a member of a team follow his leader, if he doesn't feel he belongs? Everyone desires to feel included. Even people who want to be very different from other people are conforming to certain norms.

If the leader makes people feel welcome, they will be more inclined to engage them. Being part of a group gives people a sense of security. It allows them to believe that others work with and for them.

Recognize that you too have gone through this stage and are now aspiring to leadership. You learned how important it is for someone to lean onto. Because you felt that feeling of belonging, you want it to be passed on to others.

Self-Esteem

This is Maslow's hierarchy level. It puts you next to the very top of actualization.

Who does it matter if self-esteem is required: the leader or his followers. The answer is both.

Leaders must be confident in themselves.

Why?

A leader who has low self-esteem is more likely become a bully. Fearing that someone will take his leadership down, he must find a way he can belittled. His people will also feel uncertain if he does this.

An insecure leader will micromanage. He is afraid to fail so he feels he must control everything. He cannot trust his group or the entire process.

An individual with low self-esteem is unlikely to listen to other people's opinions. He is always right. He may end up stuck in his spot, unable or unwilling to change.

A leader must have sufficient self-esteem in order to avoid all the above. He must also know how to inspire followers to do and become the same.

How does he do that, you ask?

He must make his people feel valued and respected. Not a big salary will do. For a while, it can help to soothe the hurt. It isn't something anyone wants to do. Everybody wants to feel valuable, no matter how high up they are in the hierarchy.

Self-Actualization

Imagine yourself doing what you were meant to do. You'll know it once you reach it. You will experience a happy glow that all others can see. You can inspire others to reach the same goals that you have. You have to communicate your vision.

Maslow's Hierarchy of Needs is a great resource for leaders of organizations. This will help motivate your staff.

We will start from the lowest level of the hierarchy.

Responding to Physiological Wants

Even the most loyal member has to have basic needs to survive. Leadership is nothing without followers or members. It is possible for members to leave followers if they are in danger of losing their lives or their family's.

How can you meet a person's physiological demands? These are the answers:

You must create a safe work environment.

Give them a wage that will be sufficient to pay for their physiological requirements.

Set goals that all can reach.

Each month, honor the best employees or members.

Responding to Security Issues

To function well, someone must feel safe. Imagine someone who must constantly look behind him. He will not perform as expected.

He might instead be overwhelmed by his worries.

Here are some tips to help a person with their security needs.

Maintain the position on a regular basis to create a sense of security.

You can provide a vehicle for people who don't have one, but still need to travel home late at night.

Locate the employment place or the membership in a great neighborhood.

Responding to the Need for Love and Being With Others

Leaders must understand their constituents' needs for love, belonging, and support them. If people are to feel a sense that they belong to the same organization, they will be more likely to stay with it willingly and even enthusiastically. Because he feels valued, you want him to give 100 percent. This knowledge will help him contribute more and take part in the group. It also makes him a better person.

Ensure that proper communication takes place within your organization.

Designate team-building day in the office.

Celebrate the successes of all members as a whole.

Allocate responsibility to the members of the organization.

Organise meetings to engage people in decision-making.

Name each person.

Communicate with each member individually (considering individual needs and personality).

Responding to Self Esteem Needs

A person wants to feel that he is valued and acknowledged for his accomplishments. Leadership with high self-esteem will help increase the self-esteem of his employees. He knows what it feels like to feel good. While achievements should be celebrated, failures should not always be openly discussed to others. These failures need to be discussed with the leader and each member. These failures need to be evaluated so that they don't happen again. A leader who is thoughtful and thoughtful will most likely encourage improvement among his staff.

All members, regardless their status, should be treated with respect

Recognize individual achievements publicly and privately.

Recommend a job well-done, but don't announce your failures publicly.

Reassure each person as an individual.

Responding To Self-Actualization Requirements

You're a leader looking to self-actualize. It is important that you don't hinder others on their journey to self-actualization. Everybody deserves the opportunity to be the person that they dream of being.

Offer assistance when the member is working on new tasks.

Regularly challenge each member to improve their self-esteem.

Make each task interesting (perhaps through the medium or the perceived goal).

Encourage each member to think for himself.

Do surveys to discover what motivates each person.

Offer self-development courses

Take into account the entire hierarchy pyramid. There will be issues among different levels. Some members may have the most basic of needs such as physiological. They are not ready for the greater challenges that the world has to present. They wait for someone to help with their rise.

Members who may be suffering from physiological needs

Employees and/or members at the lowest level of the organization's hierarchy (lowest salaries and support).

Volunteers with low incomes in their daytime work are less likely to be successful.

You need to be aware of people who are unable to feel secure or safe. They may be happy with their physiological needs, but they are always concerned about their physical safety.

Members who might have security concerns

Members who've been through a lot of traumas in the past

Victims who have been verbally or physically abused or sexually abused

The most vulnerable to violence in their neighbourhood

Former victim of a serious offense

Someone with a naturally fearful personality

If you are a leader who oversees a hard-working group, such as military, paramedics and police officers, it may be tempting to get tougher on your people. Even the most resilient of groups needs to have a sense belonging, trust, security and safety. This is something you, as leader, should do together with the rest of your team.

People who need to have their belongings protected

Orphans left without a parent must navigate their way through the jungle and ensure their survival.

People who have been excluded by society for any reason

Shy people who don't want to put themselves out, with other organizations

Outliers who are difficult to find a clique among the team

Newcomers (new residents, new employees, someone who moved in recently, etc.)

Your self-confidence can be improved and you will be able to encourage others to do the same. You will find that everyone is more likely to support each other when you have high self-esteem. Team members will be more likely work for each other.

People who have low self-esteem.

People who are not only shy but suffer from a lack in self-confidence

Employees who constantly self-deprecate

Those who don't know how ask for what they need.

Members who say "yes!"

It is rare that a person can reach self-actualization. This goal should be a priority for you as a leader.

Is there anyone in your team who needs self-actualization Most likely, everyone is still on their way. You, as the leader of the group, are more likely than others to still be on their way. This is precisely why you are reading this text right now.

These points apply not only to your fellow members. You might be able recognize a need within each tier of Maslow's hierarchy. Your leadership position does not protect you from being lacking in some area.

Let's take, for example, the role of leader in a non-profit. There will always be days when your body is not able to provide the funds it needs.

Reveries End-of Chapter Takeaway

This reminds you of a pastor whom I used to know as a child. He had several children. His leadership had enabled him to receive free lodgings, so he and his wife never worried about their physical needs. They also helped with everything they got. It was a continual cycle. They were able to get help, and they were also able to assist. You should know that I did not belong in their church. It's impossible to imagine me living that way. Even though I'm earning well, there are times when I wonder what my life would look like if all of it were to go wrong.

It is frightening to be stripped off your most basic needs. It's not shameful to work for your fair share.

Here's the takeaway: Everyone has different needs.

You are the one who leads.

You're the one driving the team's ship.

You need to be aware and respectful of the differences between your team members. This will allow you to respond to each person individually and authentically. The satisfaction of a team member is more than just his job. He will be happy because the company makes him feel good.

In one of my first jobs, I noticed that people who were born into financial security were more likely than those who weren't. This may seem strange until one realizes that the salaries at that company had been fixed. Others have to rush home in order to take their second job, or freelance work.

These workers were able to afford to remain behind and keep their jobs. This made them even better for their employers. Employers were simply looking at everyone the same. They didn't see beyond the time logs.

Chapter 5: The Performance Equation

The concept and practice of leadership has transformed into something more complicated. These systems can be used to increase the effectiveness of leadership in an organization. It will be difficult to achieve extraordinary performance in the workplace if these systems don't get followed, especially in difficult seasons. Statistics prove that inability to manage situations professionally has led to a decline in performance and results. These solutions can be helpful for many.

Performance Leadership is an organized, results-oriented approach in management and leadership for high-performing organisations, teams, or individuals. It is a best-practice method that drastically increases the impact and effectiveness of management and their leadership. The system increases transparency, integrity and accountability across the organization. It results in better reproducibility of strategic priorities being deployed, more efficient operations and increased stakeholder happiness.

Performance Leadership provides the chance to gain the edge through the development of the core roles necessary for management and leadership teams to achieve high efficacy. Simply, it is about working smarter in order to create the conditions that allow you to succeed. In contrast, those who are least productive put all their effort into supporting operational results. These results indicate that performance equation is the best method to lead performance.

WHAT IS PERFORMANCEEQUATION?

Performance equation says that leadership performance is always a function between talent and motivation. It is the result of the interaction of motivation, talent, support. Each component is vital in helping a company or its workers to achieve their goals. Importantly, all three components of the Performance Equation must work together to discourage people from inspiring or compromising their mental values.

The three pieces together make the cookie incredible. In order to make people feel good about coming into work, they must all be part of the performance equation.

Performance Leadership is the most important commodity and cannot be underemphasized. It is the connection between the set and ability for leaders to relate freely and responsible to one another, and perform optimally. Leadership is not an opportunity to place your preconceived ideas and tactics on the team. It's about providing visionary or change leadership, building trust, and building business relationships.

If an executive is not performing at an acceptable pace or trend, they will often mention environmental factors. "If only CEOs were more proactive," and "My role in decision making is not defined and causes confusion." The concept engagement is more nuanced than the introvert/extrovert distinction or the raft on environmental factors outlined above. These can be valid assessments of the state-of-play or executive projects blame for inability or unwillingness to adapt.

It is crucial that you remember that performance management is the string-up for highlighting the positive and minimizing the negative aspects of the work environment. Command connects the situation of the organization with the "can and will do" aspects and personality of the individual, the "will fit," in order to foster engagement and resourcefulness.

Positive management commitment will lead to intrinsic satisfaction, high motivation, and excellent employment and operational performance. Organizations will continue to evolve. It is essential that organizations develop and maintain a core of talented managers who are capable of leading, engaging, building culture, shaping the company for the long-term in light new challenges and opportunities.

It is important to be clear about your roles and design them accordingly. It is not possible to establish an appraisal framework if the foundation is weak. Interaction between business strategy as well the role and quantum of financial and other rewards is critical.

It's not worth offering a highly competitive incentive-based compensation plan to our performance manager if that individual only wants to attend the next conference related to industry-specific skills and knowledge. Good performance management allows for meaningful employer-executive interaction, and intelligent career administration.

LEWIN'S PRANFORMANCE EQUATION

Lewin is the original father of the performance formula. While its utility has not been fully developed, his work was the foundation for the revolution in performance leadership. Lewin suggested equation B=f (P x e) in 1936. But he didn't explain how the interaction between the individual and the environment would work. Below is an extended and more organizationally lucidized interpretation of Lewin's original model.

From an organizational standpoint, the core concept of the model is the archaic adage "Can do, Will do, Will Fit". However, the model expands upon this to illustrate the factors that help to fuel this basic proposition.

The most important aspect of the model is employee engagement. Before we get to that point, however, we need to know the person's attributes. They include appropriate levels and abilities, knowledge and experience, cognitive strength and flexibility, as well as aligned familiarity. They can also be evaluated by essential job matching and operational assessment ability testing. You can make your team stronger by carefully considering all these factors.

Even more important, if the person you are looking for is a good fit with your values, culture and leadership, and stays aligned over time, they will likely be a better fit. You should use valid psychological assessment tools to evaluate your temperament, emotional flexibility as well as strength.

STATISTICS HEARS ABOUT MOTORIZATION

Managers are expected to motivate their employees as a key function of their leadership. This is according to a survey that was done using managers who had experience in performance leadership. 94% of managers believe that motivating their employees is vital to the success in their business.

82% of managers feel that their behavior can have a significant affect on their motivation. Yet, here's what managers have to face lately: 68% say it is getting more difficult to motivate employees. This shows that even though leaders know they need to do this, significant numbers of them are still struggling with the metamorphosis in human nature and wants.

MOTIVATION EQUATION AND PERFORMANCE

The definition of motivation can vary depending on the perspective and insight. It can range from the pure inner drive, to the complex. A set of intrinsic or extrinsic variables that allows for abnormal human behavior in order to attain results that satisfy any desire or need. Motivation is the inner driving force, passion, energy, and energy of someone.

It is important to recognize that our inner drive, and energy, can be significantly affected by the surrounding environment. Therefore, the role of the environment in performance should not be underestimated. It is also possible to influence motivation through isolation. The right motivation is what will make anyone feel inspired. People often think of motivation as the key to governing performance because it is sourced from the inner desire to make things work. Everyone believes that motivation is what motivates people to work harder. This belief also holds true for people who believe that hard work will pay off.

The leader who is results-oriented will take extra care to ensure that all employees have the skills and knowledge necessary to succeed in the organization. Talent refers specifically to the ability of a person to perform the job efficiently. This is because it's possible to cultivate understanding and expertise. The process of hiring employees was very well established in the organizations that we reviewed. We were able take on their employees, and to lead them to their work.

They were committed to ensuring their workers were well-suited to their job and had made training and growth an integral part their corporate culture.

These examples resulted a talented workforce equipped with the skills needed to succeed. Performance equations help employees motivate in precise, realistic and holistic ways. Employees have to be able understand their vision, tasks, and expectations. They set goals and expectations for each worker so they know what to expect. This type leadership fosters employee decision making, participation, empowerment, and honors all employees.

Such companies will provide feedback and continuous coaching to their employees in order to help them grow professionally. In addition, they establish effective incentive systems that help their employees see the important link between their performance and the rewards they receive.

The performance leadership formula enhances support for their employees. It is clear that they made every effort to keep their employees informed about both company performance and internal decisions. They also created systems that would quickly eliminate performance barriers and address any potential problems that could hinder performance. These systems of leadership take great care to provide effective leadership to their employees as well as to foster the development of both the workforce, and the management teams. Great companies don't just focus on employee motivation. They also created an organizational culture and climate that encouraged the best out of their employees.

If you don't have a deep understanding of how people think, managing a team can be very difficult. You must motivate your team members to make it a success. More people seek affirmation, and they are feeling lost in their work. They want validation and to feel heard. But, most importantly, they want the assurance that their contributions are being recognized and appreciated.

Not because they want to be noticed but because they care about their ability to make an impact on the future of the organizations that they serve. Do not tell your employees that they need to perform better. Most people believe your selfish ambition to achieve a competitive advantage is what drove you to say this. Instead, show your employees why their contributions contribute to the company's growth and solve problems. It is more motivating for team members to do their best when they realize that their work has value for the entire organization.

For instance, I would always be able to show my team the results of their collective efforts. To see new labeled products on the shelves we'd go to the factory and either watch the product being produced or look at it in action in the store. By recognizing the commitment of your team members, you can instill performance and connect the dots. It's about more than just what you can offer. It's about what the group will do along the way.

It is frightening to see some organizations flourish while the team that is responsible for the success of the unit is not. You can help your team or employees be successful. This is a key aspect of the performance equation. Employees don't want to feel low about the company's achievements. Leaders are responsible for generating meaning in their lives and making their job more rewarding. Each employee's performance should be measured in two areas. Achievement and importance. Let's take sales as an example of a category of results. Your employee was able to complete 90 percent of this program. That's great. Measure the significance of the sales once you've discussed how to reach 100%.

The plan might have generated 90 percent revenue, which could be enough to hire five people more or provide funding for a specific community outreach program. This is possible because of local market forces. The importance of the success or failure of another individual is unknown until you do an evaluation. Therefore, it is possible to promote even more success by promoting respect. Not only should you show gratitude and encouragement but also respect the work of your employees. Respect must be built. People want to know they are valued.

Recognition addicts are common in the workplace. It is because they feel insecure about their contribution to the system. In an era of extreme rivalry, it became our belief that we were our own friend. We believe we are all dependent on each other.

We must market ourselves better than any other person, regardless of the suggestions or opinions made by others. This attitude jeopardizes our long-term careers. It is sad that so many people want attention but forget that getting respect is much more important. It is important to retrain your employees and guide them on how respect can be achieved. They will be inspired by you if they see the bigger impact respect has.

Chapter 6: Individual Decision Making

Here's a brief overview of the major theories that explain why people are motivated. A leader needs to be able understand the processes behind decisions, both at an individual level as well as in a group setting. We make most of the decisions that we make as individuals. We will start with the most common approaches that people take when making decisions.

Simon Herbert, a prolific scholar with over 1,000 publications came up with a 1947 definition that included intelligence gathering and design. He realized that no amount information gathering could provide complete intelligence, so he proposed the theory of bound rationality. Our rationality depends on the information we have. At the other end, information overload can cause us to forget or not process enough information. This is just as the case when we have too much information. As a result, we turn to heuristics and shortcuts to help us make decisions. Leaders need to be aware and sensitive to the biases inherent in our natural desire to make information more accessible. As a simple example, an employee who feels overwhelmed by too much information may take shortcuts and assume that an employee with less information is the same.

Let's see some other examples frequented by business leaders.

Anchoring: It's a common tactic for negotiation. The first offer anchors a negotiation to a specific level. After that, adjustments are made. The same goes for anchoring. In a sea filled with information, we can either choose to focus on one number, concept, or fact or infer something from very little. Then we adjust that anchor using new information. But, we already believe the truth to be close. Sometimes business managers anchor employees' opinions on their strengths and weaknesses. Then they make small adjustments over time. This is why it's important to get a first impression, regardless of whether you're new or experienced.

The Concise Reads The Art of Negotiation is our best-selling book on anchoring.

Naive diversification: A leader who is faced with many choices but has limited information or doesn't understand all of them fully, tends to select choices that are consistent and aligned with multiple strategies instead of a single strategy. If this happens, you will need more information before you can make a better decision. It's not necessary to employ multiple strategies hoping that one of them hits the mark.

Sunk Cost Fault: Also known as Escalation of Commitment or Escalation of Commitment, this phenomenon states that the most common reason someone makes a choice is because they have made it before. Managers who have invested in a project are more likely to continue to do so, despite increased costs and decreased revenues. They are more likely to choose a different strategy because they have invested (psychologically). Also known to be Gambler's error.

These concepts can be used when you evaluate your own decisions and those of your employees.

GROUP DECISION MAKING

"The conflict and disagreement of differing opinions can lead to the wrong decision. However, the right understanding comes from the consideration of all possible alternatives."

Peter Drucker

It is not a decision-making tool. It allows you to use the power that group dynamics can provide to create as many creative solutions as possible. Andre Delbecq developed the technique with Andrew H. Van de V. It involves first gathering your team. After that, you'll need to solve problems and decide on a solution. It may seem similar to brainstorming and then having a vote. The real difference lies in the way that votes are tallied. The method used to rank the votes is different for each member of the group. They then give their own solutions to the problem. NGT has been used by think tanks as well as other groups like IDEO (product design company IDEO), to teach the important lesson of divergence and convergence. In other words: you want to generate the most solutions possible. You should encourage everyone to participate in brainstorming and then allow for discussion to potentially mix and match solutions. After everything is said, convergence occurs and a solution can be chosen.

NGT can be used to generate more solutions, according to research. Participation from all members is also proven to lead to greater satisfaction and achievement in the group meeting.

Value-Driven design (VDD) is a process that allows many disciplines to come together and find solutions to multidisciplinary problems. James Sturges, Lockheed Martin, was the first to coin it. It was used then by the American Institute of Aeronautics and Astronautics. It is often interchangeable with the US Defense Advanced Research Projects Agency model of Value-Centric-Design. Agile software engineering is a model similar to the one used in the digital world. Instead of getting bogged down by performance metrics, all three prioritize the most valuable aspects of a project and prioritize work. It allows designers to be more efficient and focuses attention on the most critical tasks. First, a model of value is created. It is an objective function that ranks which items would add the most economic value to the final product. This is an objective valuation model. This is an objective value model. The design process involves considering several options. Each attribute is then sacrificed to gain additional resources. The total score is then calculated from the ranking. This is slightly different from the Multi Attribute Utility model (or MAU model), which builds a subjective model of utility based off the utility to various stakeholders.

Multi-Attribute Universal Model (MAU), where we are required to build a utility model that is based upon agreed upon criteria. Next is to provide alternative solutions. We do this again when we consider the possibility of future changes to the criteria. Both scenarios allow us to test alternative solutions against the criteria.

The templates and frameworks available online for group decision making are robust. Your goal will dictate whether VDD or MAU is used. Does it maximize economic value (and therefore profit) or maximize the utility of the stakeholders involved, whether they are clients or partners? The framework allows a group to design with purpose rather than just designing the best product. This requires input by everyone in the room, just like our Nominal Group Theory.

The industry has a term that refers to outsourcing the design process, but wanting control over the criteria. These specifications are most often seen in government contracts that involve service or product design companies. This is Value Based Acquisition. This is more appropriate if your organization doesn't have the necessary expertise but understands the criteria.

These are some of the main methods for group decisions, with NGT being the most used in management meetings. John F. Kennedy used this very technique when creating a team with experts to handle the Cuban missile crisis.

Chapter 7: The Skills Of A Leader

Young leaders must develop the emotional and psychological strength to communicate well with investors, high-ranking managers, and tough competitors. Leaders should have big ideas and demonstrate conviction.

For a new leader, the art of command will be a crucial skill. This means a leader will be unpopular when necessary, confronting adversity headon and encouraging open discussion to help solve tough problems and crises.

Don't be afraid to be yourself. This is a wonderful skill for a new leader. Remember, your attitude and reputation are both yours. "BE YOURSELF" - Express instead of impress.

What are the ABC skills that a new leader should have?

"A" stands For Attitude

Success or failure is determined more by how you think than your mental abilities. Only 5% of people do well, while 95% of them fail. This is not because you have talent or money. The answer is attitude. You can't achieve the results you want or maintain your position of leader if you don't have a positive outlook.

Attitudes drive behavior. Your mental attitude will affect how you feel about your body. Your attitude determines how you behave and the message it sends. You can choose the attitude you wish to adopt almost every time. There is no set way to behave in work situations. For example, if you feel angry about something happening, that is the way you should feel. The event does not require you to feel the way you do. It's up to you. You do have the choice. It's your decision.

As we live longer, the more we see the impact of our attitude on how we live. Attitude is far more important than facts. It is important more than education, past experiences, money, circumstances and success. And it is more important to us than what other people think or do. It is even more important than the appearance, gift or skill. It could be what makes or breaks a business, person, church, or house.

Amazingly, every day is a decision day. We have the option to choose what attitude and how we behave. We cannot change our past. People will continue to act the same way. The unavoidable is what we cannot change. The only thing we can control is the attitude we adopt.

I believe that life is only 10 percent what happens, and 90 percent what I do with it. As it is for you. We can control our attitudes. - Charles Swindoll

How can you have a positive attitude and develop it? It all boils down to what you choose.

Evaluate your current attitude. While self-evaluation might not be easy, it is one of the most effective routes to self discovery.

You can have faith, even if you fear it. You can be positive, and you should seek out positive reinforcement.

Desire to change?

We tend to only change when there is a massive boulder in our path. But your attitude and willingness to change will determine whether you succeed. Begin by stepping out of your comfort zone. Take it step by step.

You can develop habits that are either good or bad. Mindfulness is the key to developing a good habit. Your attitude will be affected if you have bad habits. List bad habits to identify the source. Choose a positive habit to replace it. This habit can be strengthened by daily action. Reward yourself for your efforts. Once you have established new habits, you'll be ready for new challenges. They need to be associated and made with the right decisions.

Always choose the right attitude. You only need to wish for things that will be beneficial to you. Wishing for the best is free. Attitudes are often not able to change. The most challenging stages are often those at the beginning. Old habits die hard. Mentally, you must guard yourself.

Every person in every situation is a leader. Even though you may lack the prestige and salary that you deserve, it is not impossible to assume some leadership responsibilities. It is rare for leaders to rise to the top. They start from the bottom and work up. They possess strong leadership traits that distinguish them from the rest. We all have different leadership styles, and not everyone is a natural leader.

We have control over our thoughts. However, our emotions are influenced by our thoughts.

"B", for Behaviour

Evidence shows that improving any leadership behavior will have a positive impact on team satisfaction/commitment.

"I have three valuable things that I treasure and hold close to my heart. The first is gentleness. The second is frugality. And the third is humility. I don't want to put myself ahead of others. Be gentle, and you have the potential to be bold; be frugal, and you could be generous; avoid putting others before yourself and you might become a leader. --Lao Tzu

Mullins (2007) defines only leadership as: A relationship in which one person can influence the behavior or action of others.

Leadership means facing difficult situations head-on. In general, there are only two ways to resolve difficulties.

You can either try to change the circumstances or you can stay the same.

Resolve to do better in dealing with the difficult circumstances.

You can learn to deal with difficult situations and benefit from your experience, or worse yet, that of others, to improve your confidence.

Your team and you must set high expectations. Responsible for setting or helping to achieve the appropriate goals and objectives. In order to achieve success, overcomes obstacles

Jack Welch from General Electric is a great businessman. Welch knew that he had to transform everything in order to drive GE to new heights. This is exactly what Welch did.

He came up with the concept of a "boundaryless" organization. This means everyone has the freedom to brainstorm and to come up with new ideas, instead of waiting for someone else in the bureaucracy.

He wanted his employees to be open-minded and would listen to any ideas from them. He did. Everyone, from the lowest-ranking workers to the most senior management, received his attention. He wanted to know if anyone had a suggestion or something to add that would improve the company. His team quickly figured out that it was not just talk.

Welch believed in his passions, and did not compromise on what was right. Under his leadership, GE became a very successful company. His team was willing and able to follow his lead as they understood that he never faltered.

What does that mean for me? If you show your team that you care and are open to learning, then they'll most likely follow you.

Lead by example creates a positive image of what is possible. People can look up at you and see that you can do anything. It's easier for others follow your example if you are a leader.

Look around at the amazing people who changed the world by their actions. Mahatma Mahatma was an example of what you can do when you live what you preach to others.

People followed his example and supported nonviolent resistance against injustice. He led India, as well as them, to independence, because of his example.

A leader's job is to inspire people to strive for greatness. You can only do this by leading them.

How can you help your team develop and support each other?

Create sustainable processes to support growth: Leaders should expect to mentor and develop their teams. At the very least, everyone should know where they need improvement. For those with exceptional potential, career tracks can be created to give them an idea of their future.

Make problems an opportunity for learning and development in real life. Your team members can identify challenges where they might be able to grow. Learning organizations see challenges as opportunities. It is important to reinforce the value and importance of learning. Be more than a baseline conversation about your goals. Ask them what they want to achieve and where their gaps lie. You should celebrate the accomplishment of an assignment.

Teams should be able connect their everyday tasks and responsibilities with the values of the organization. They need to be able understand why the work they do is important.

"A leader takes people to places they would never have gone on their own." -Hans Finzel

Leaders are only more powerful when they are seen to be learning. It is important to be honest about the need to learn, and how you can help others.

How well you train and develop your staff is an important factor in the performance of a group.

Training and development are essential for individuals in order to improve their effectiveness and tackle more complex and important problems. Not only do they need ongoing training and development, but they also need support in learning new skills as the work environment changes.

"The greatest leader may not necessarily be the one who does great things. He is responsible for getting people to do the best things. Ronald Reagan

Talk the Talk

Be determined for results. You need to not only support your team but also develop them and deal with problems head on. You should view setbacks more as a challenge than a problem or issue. Setbacks can be part of everyday life. If you experience setbacks, you should not feel embarrassed. Do not take it personally. Instead, learn from it and move on.

It is important to be open and honest about what happened. Be honest about the circumstances. Be positive and don't get discouraged when setbacks occur.

You can turn setbacks and disappointments into development opportunities by asking for positive questions, such:

What are some positive things about this situation

How can you make the most of this situation. What can it teach me?

What is the truth behind this problem

How can this be avoided next time?

Steps to Overcome Any Obstacles That Keep You Back

Be gentler and more kind to yourself than your inner critic. This voice can be used to promote positivity and forward momentum.

Imagine your life as if you do nothing.

You can keep an ongoing record of your goal(s).

Note down any excuses you have used to hold yourself back. Now take a hard look at the excuses. Identify the "excuses" that are valid. You can then create an action strategy and begin to implement it.

Include dates for when you wish to achieve each goal.

"You must be passionate about an idea, problem or wrong you want to rectify. You'll never be passionate enough to start the project. - Steve Jobs

"The ultimate measurement of a man does not depend on his standing in moments of comfort. He must stand when there is challenge and controversy. Martin Luther King, Jr.

"C" is for Character

Martin Luther King Jr., a late civil rights leader, advised his followers that they should not judge people based on their appearance but the content of their character.

A person's character, whether it is good or bad can inspire others or discourage them.

The most authentic leaders have strong, personal moral values. This can have a profound impact on their team. How character impacts your organization and your team, and how it can help you attract the best.

Leaders of character show genuine concern for the people they work with. While it is important to keep a distance between work and personal relationships, it is equally important to show concern for others.

Character is the essence of who we really are when no one else is looking.

Leadership is an honor and comes with many obligations. For example, leaders must instill trust that people will do the right thing regardless of being watched.

Kevin Cashman, the late Kevin Cashman makes a powerful distinction among character, the essence and who we are. And persona, our external personality created to handle everyday life.

A leader who models authenticity is one who guides by character, while a leader who model personality is one who inspires by image.

A leader who leads by character values creating value and adding to the community, not winning at all cost. This leader values openness, inclusion, and avoids control and exclusion.

Excellence brings responsibility. Leaders take full responsibility for their actions, even if this means making mistakes. They have a strong sense for accountability and expect the same of their team members.

Here Are A Few Tips To Inspire You In Your Leadership Journey

Make Values a Reality: Making your values a reality is one of the most important aspects of character.

Be known as A Promise-Keeper: Authors Barry Posner, James Kouzes, and Barry Posner discuss the Leadership Challenge's "Model the Way" concept. They offer personal examples to illustrate this. Keep your promises, and do what you promise. No matter how small the promises may be, regardless of who they are made to, it is important to keep your word. Even though we may not be able to keep our promises due to circumstances, don't let that happen. Get back to everyone to tell them why. Keep your word as valuable currency and see how you value your words.

Don't Cut corners on Quality: Henry Ford said, "Quality means doing the right thing when no one is looking." Are you a leader who insists that quality is important, but then tells people to do things quickly to avoid quality. Your credibility is eroded when you do this. They will eventually discount quality if you speak about it as lip service.

Be consistent in how you deal with others. Is it possible to complain unwittingly about someone on your team to other members of your team? It is easy for us to get complacent, especially when we are frustrated by the day.

Audit Your Decisions

A concern about our reputation is one of the reasons why we are more civilized if we know we're being watched. Reputation refers only to the quality of our character or character. It is the layer that others see.

To be a leader, you must have compassion. In business, the heart can be difficult to discuss because people will feel like they are being "walked all over" when they show compassion. True compassion and heart is not soft.

Without compassion and releasing judgments, one cannot really see another person. You must be a clear leader. If a leader has preconceived ideas about people, situations and people, they make it impossible for others to rise up to the occasion.

Coachability: Keep learning. Do not let your guard down or feel insufficient. Always look for ways you can improve.

Learn how to lead a pack from wild dogs or a pride from lions.

The pride will not concentrate on one specific area in the forest when the pack is looking for a hunt.

Different members may look in various directions to spot prey. Once a prey is found, each member will move swiftly together towards it. They must follow the following simple rule until they have enough prey.

During the hunting operation, there are different leaders who lead the team. They don't fight. After stocking the prey, the key hunter would move calmly and take a break while the rest of the team would begin to eat it.

Groups of likeminded people can turn ambitious plans into reality. These people share the same objective, outlook, and passion. Leadership requires teamwork.

Some leaders choose to lead from an arrogant and domineering "top down" model because it is traditional, more common, easier, and comes naturally.

This leadership style may not work well to create a conducive environment that fosters collaboration and productivity. It may not also be the most efficient form of leadership for making an organisation more efficient and furthering its mission and vision.

Encouragement of team members to think independently is believed to improve organizations' innovative capabilities (Nederveen und al., 2010).

Garcia-Morales et.al., 2007, found that team members can be empowered to think and act independently and this reduces barriers for knowledge sharing and utilization within an organization (Garcia Morales et.al., 2007).

A clear understanding of the connections between the tasks/values assigned to team members and the vision/values for the organization can increase individual motivation (Wolfram&Mohr, 2009).

There appears to be a direct correlation between the leader's ability and commitment to team members (Bass (2006)).

Team members that are empowered and encouraged to take on challenging projects and to develop their skills has been proven to be a key factor in project success (Prabhakar. 2005).

Ayoko & Callan, 2010, showed that encouraging and enthusiastic communication about the organization's vision can increase team cohesion.

Chapter 8: Authority Eats First. Leaders Eat Last

"Leaders have to be willing to look out both for those on the left and the right. Leaders will be willing to sacrifice their own interests for others. Their time, their energy and even their money. Leaders choose to eat the last meal when it's important."

--Simon Sinek

Simon Sinek (author of WHY LAWFUL LEADERS EAT LASTS) describes himself to be an unshakeable optimist and believes in the possibility that we can create a brighter, better future. Sinek interviewed three-star Marine Corps General to help him research his book on leadership. During the conversation, Sinek asked the Marine Corps general "What makes them so good at what we do?". The general answered with three simple words: Officers eat last.

Marines line-up in rank order in every Marine base, anywhere in the globe, at food halls. Although seniority can allow people to eat before others, the best leaders won't. Sinek explains that leadership comes at the cost of self-interest in one of his thoughtful talks on what makes great leaders. If you aren't willing to give up your perks whenever it matters, then you should not be promoted. You might be an authority, however, you will not be a leader" (Sinek (2018)

Leadership: The Unusualness of Leadership

You are the leader. People congratulate you when things are going great, but when things don't turn out so well, they all blame you. It doesn't matter what role you played in that specific success (although that is a plus as a leader). What matters, however, is that as the leader you have signed an unspoken contract to your followers. As the leader you have the responsibility to speak up and, if necessary take the fall on behalf of the team. Sinek defines this as the anthropological meaning of a leader.

The Alpha Eats First...Until That Matters

We usually let people who display greater alpha qualities than ourselves take over the authority role when we come across them. Alpha is the Greek alphabet's first letter. It is used as a term to describe people who are more powerful than us. Alphas are allowed to eat first in nature.

The female lions are the ones who do all of the work during hunts. They work together to coordinate an action plan and then execute it to perfection. This ensures that their pride is well fed. When it comes time for the hunt, the female hunters allow the alpha men to eat first. It doesn't have to be the alpha male in human society. However, the same rules apply. Sinek said that "Alphas get the first choice between meat and mate."

Leaders can not only get in the queue at the naked sushi restaurant, but there are also other benefits. People will offer their help, guide you and provide preferential treatment. Leadership makes you feel like a boss or king. It's meant to. Because there is another side to leadership. When things don't go according to plan and external threats threaten your group, people who have given this preferential treatment expect that you deal with them. You are more powerful, well-paid, healthier, and confident than anyone in the group. We expect our leaders to run with all their might towards danger to protect ourselves.

Sinek said that medals in the military are awarded to those who have sacrificed their lives so that others might gain. We give bonuses to people willing to sacrifice so that leaders may win in business. This is how it works.

The Leader: A Motivational Speaker

Simon Sinek is an example of a motivator who views themselves as a leader. Why? Because they're leading the way to a brighter day. They are actively encouraging millions of people to strive for leadership and inspire them to do so. Motivating others through motivational speaking and developing leadership skills are inextricably linked. It is the easiest way for someone to motivate themselves to become a leader in your own life. Also, the reverse is true. All great leaders practice and improve their motivational speaking and public speaking skills. Don't believe us? We have five reasons to believe that it is crucial for great leaders to learn the skills of motivational speakers (Rangwala 2017)

Be a force for unity with a shared vision

The root of the term motivational speaker is found in the first sentence. It refers to people who can inspire leadership through speeches and public speaking. By focusing on your motivations, you can create a vision that your entire team can see. If you are passionate about motivating your team, then it is worth the effort.

Encourage positive change

Your organization must be open about the changes they want and then motivate people to implement them. Email is not enough. Your team must be gathered together and delivered a speech. This will inform and motivate them to make the desired changes. Make sure to follow up with your team regularly to keep them on track. Research has shown that people are more likely to change when they hear it in person than if they receive it via text message, phone or email.

Get closer to your audience

Show your commitment to helping your team succeed if you want to win them over. Your audience will be impressed if you communicate with them often in a sincere, open, and confident fashion. Your personal social media accounts should be updated regularly so that your audience feels connected to your progress. If you are unsure about how to reach your target audience, you need to reconsider your leadership style. A holistic approach will include all aspects of an organization that contribute to its success.

Build a Following

A group of followers that don't follow a leader is similar to a hand with no thumb. In the same way, a leader with no followers is like a thumb and a hand without a hand. It is essential for a leader that they grow their followers. The best way to achieve this is to be comfortable in front your potential and current supporters and inspire them to share your vision. Your followers won't recognize you if your confidence is lacking in standing before them and giving a motivational talk. If you want to grow your following, you must be visible. You need to speak up in front and express your vision with pride, conviction, and clarity.

Your Followers are Your Friends

Public speaking and motivational speeches are key tools to help leaders get their message across. Humans live for stories. Some people even claim stories are what make us humans. If a storyteller has mastered the art of storytelling, it is hard not to be moved, captivated, and even intrigued by a story. Stories make us FEEL. And that's why the best leaders are great motivational speakers and skilled storytellers--because that's the way to win over not just the minds of your followers, but the hearts, too.

Motivations for Leaders

Motivation is your reason for doing something or being a certain way. Motivation is a goal-oriented characteristic. It means that you should set goals if your motivation is to succeed in completing a task. If you think your motivation is getting a six-pack from hard work, it is likely that this is what you will achieve. This is not the case. We are looking at motivation through the lens of the attribute that helps someone achieve their goals. We've looked at how leaders motivate others. But what makes a leader a motivator?

Simon Sinek (and many other leaders of today) would suggest that leadership should not be used solely to motivate others. The following are guidelines on how to view the motivations and strengths of a good leader. (Juneja, 2015).

Harmonize your Morals, and Ethics

Good leaders should be the embodiments of their organization. As mentioned in the book, great leaders walk their walk and live their words. This means the morals & ethics of the leader reflect the morals & ethics of their organization. Leaders must always be motivated and inspired to be the best they can be, in order to represent the best within their organization.

Reward excellence, even your own!

Sometimes, it is easy to praise everyone else's successes as a leader. However, you should always look critically at your own accomplishments. Progress can be a tricky thing, especially when you're as invested in her as you are in yourself. When you achieve a significant "win", reward your team's performance with little tokens.

Role model status is Motivation enough

If you already possess the qualities and characteristics of an effective leader or are actively learning them, then you are well on your path to becoming a rolemodel for your colleagues and society as a whole. Because that is what leaders do. I will share a secret with y'all: Being a rolemodel makes you, as a leader, feel great. It makes you feel valuable and that's why you should keep improving as a leader. What a motivating feeling when your followers accomplish their goals and are eager to come to celebrate with you.

Does a leader require freedom?

As I mentioned, the motivations of a leader are, in large part, the feeling of motivating others. You have to harmonize your morals with the organization's ethics, reward yourself for high performance, and be a leader that epitomizes "leadership." The next question is: DO LEADERS NEED FREEDOM

What is Freedom to Leaders?

Freedom is often described as having the freedom to act or change without limitation. This definition implies that a leader cannot be free. However, this is only a part of freedom. The definition also states that freedom refers to a person's ability and willingness to achieve their goals, wants, and needs. It seems that freedom should be the aspiration for all great leaders.

Just as the donkey had the carrot dangling before its face, it was a motivator to keep it moving forward. The same can be said for freedom when it comes down to leadership. With the carrot hanging, the donkey was able to go farther than it would had it not gotten the carrot at all. The donkey carried the man (a metaphor for you team) farther than either of them thought possible. The carrot of freedom is the metaphor you use. But, what if that carrot were yours and you could enjoy the flavors? Would you then be back to the forefront of the path with the same determination as before.

The question is: WHAT RIGHTS DOES A LEADER HAVE? Of a certain type, yes. A leader must have the ability to decide and act on behalf of the organization. They need to be able lead their team the best way possible. Leaders must balance their freedom with the responsibility they have for the position they hold. Uncle Ben said that "With great power comes great obligation."

Chapter 9: The Ability To Decide On Tough Issues

Martin O'Malley. "Leadership consists of making the right and best decisions before it becomes all popular."

If a group is to be successful, it is vital for the majority (if not all) of its members to work in the exact same direction. That can only be achieved if only one person has the power and responsibility of making decisions. That's you, the leader.

If this is not the situation, a group can become overwhelmed and end up with "too much cooks that spoil their broth." A group that tries to take the group in two directions is likely. This can hinder its ability to move forward or cause them to split. Either way, the group won't reach its goals.

To be a leader, you must have the ability to make difficult decisions. It's not difficult to make low-risk but high-success decision. It is much easier to be responsible for easy decisions that result in success. It can be very difficult when you have to make tough decisions that might not be liked by the group or have serious repercussions. Sometimes, leaders are faced with difficult situations. These are sometimes necessary for achieving goals and objectives.

Fear of failing is one of many reasons people find it difficult to make difficult decisions. Fear of failure is a common fear. This is because people are unable to take into account probabilities and plan for possible consequences. There are many ways to combat this fear.

Charles Duhigg, a best-selling author, describes "probabilistic-thinking" as a way to make difficult choices easier. It is used to help people avoid the fallacy, that all options are acceptable if they have a 100% probability of success.

Such thinking is a fallacy. It is not possible to be certain of anything in this world. All start up businesses run the risk of failing to survive beyond their first year. This is not up for discussion. While some start up businesses have very little risk, others have very high.

Many of the largest and longest-lasting companies in the world were founded small. They knew there were risks and that their businesses might fail. Only the difference is that they believed that such risks are low and that there were high chances of their start-up businesses succeeding.

Others, however, are able to choose to work in the corporate sector instead of following their passions fully because they were confident that they would be able earn a living by following their passions.

Probabilistic thinking is a way to accept the fact that you may not get the results you want. If such risks seem low, however, probability thinking can help with tough decisions.

Making tough decisions can be made easier by learning to balance the costs and benefits of not making them. Because of their costs as well the repercussions, certain decisions can be very difficult. Sometimes, leaders do not realize the consequences and costs of difficult decisions.

But there are some costs to not making the decision. To save money every month for retirement, it can be challenging because it could require cutting down on things you enjoy or enjoying, like dining out or watching movies every weekend. Those are decision-making costs.

You can't avoid making tough decisions about cutting down on recreation and saving money to invest or for emergency purposes, such as hospitalization. There's also a price. It's not having enough to save for retirement, for medicines, or to be admitted when you get sick.

It is possible to change your outlook on difficult or important decisions by being aware of both the costs and benefits of skipping them. It is possible to change your perspective and make it easier for yourself to make such difficult decisions. When you realize the price of not making tough decisions outweighs the benefit of making them, you will feel more motivated and stronger to make them.

Learning to anticipate and plan for the possible consequences of tough decisions can help you make better decisions. For example, if you must make the difficult decision of firing someone because of work-related redundancy, you can minimize the impact on that employee by giving him referrals within the company and other organizations. Also, you can give him a 30-45-day period to allow him to search for work while still making a living.

Chapter 10: Communicator

People have never complained about being too well-informed. Has anyone ever been fired for being "way too well informed?" Is it possible to complain about transparency and involvement within a company? Not that I know of.

I've experienced much of the opposite. "No one understands what's happening here", "noone can tell me anything"," "I'm always lost." Sound familiar? That's what I thought.

Communication is critical to the success of any organization. Employees must be able communicate with each other daily to understand where they're going and why.

You Talky as the Leader

Yes, it's true. Managers will have to talk. Your style doesn't really matter so long it informs. You are the gatekeeper for information about your team. It's up you to decide whether you want be a waterfall or a funnel.

Individual

Individual communication will be your first level. Clear, concise, understandable and relatable communication is essential. This is the first thing that you will need, and it may seem contradictory. I have already mentioned Chapter 3...empathetic Listening. That's right. To communicate effectively, you must first listen. Listening helps you understand your audience and then how to connect to them.

Think about your point before you deliver a message. This will make it easier to handle any criticisms, questions or concerns. Because this will allow you to redirect your attention back to the main purpose of the message.

If you give constructive feedback, then you can tell your team member you care. But what they are doing right now isn't great performance and ultimately holds everyone back. Although this may sound harsh, it is important to understand. I was shocked to find out that 2/3rd of managers are not comfortable communicating with employees.

It is no surprise that many people feel uninformed. If we don't, who will?

As people leaders, we have to be willing to communicate with our staff members no matter what it takes. They will understand that you care about your team and will respond accordingly if your intent is to serve, help, and care for them.

Group

I don't know this for sure, but I'm willing to bet that public speaking has to be one of the greatest fears. As the manager, you don't have this luxury. You must address all the members of your team in a group setting. It is likely that you will be doing this quite frequently.

It is, however, quite similar to individual communication in many aspects. Knowing your audience and understanding what motivates, inspires and suits them is the first step. Once you understand these things, you can tailor your message better to address those needs while also sharing some information that may be of use to you.

You need to plan well and be prepared for group communication. Your key thoughts and themes should be written down.

It's that easy! I did some acting during college and highschool, but I didn't know how useful it was in helping me to communicate with others. You can draw from any of these experiences to increase your confidence and skill in public speaking.

To Build A Communication Ecosystem

You can't be the only person talking. In order to have a well informed team and organization, you need to establish a network of talkers.

Platforms

Email, phone, meetings, huddles and communication boards. You can accomplish all of these and you'll be fine.

Drop mic.

Kidding, of course. A lot of leaders are asking me, which one is better? The answer is that they all work well together! All three can be used at the same time, for different purposes by different people. Let your team decide what works for them. You will have more people using the tools you choose and how to use them.

You'll likely need to do most of your heavy lifting first before you can use the platforms, especially newer ones, until more people take up the challenge.

The last organization I led had a Facebook group. One would assume that they would immediately jump on it with a predominantly younger crowd. They had to recognize that it was safe. When I and my leadership team began posting regularly, it soon took root. It helped dramatically improve communication between the various departments and made the organization feel smaller.

Habits

This is the most important. The most important thing is that people can learn more about themselves and their surroundings on their own. Sally sharing with Bob the latest happenings in another area of the team, organization, or company is fine, unless you are a micromanaging, control freak manager. It's not necessary for it to go through your eyes.

If you can get your team to share more information and communication, it will be second nature.

Charles Duhigg[19] just released The Power of Habit. Paul shared a story in the book about Alcoa. It started by focusing on safety habits, and ended up transforming all other aspects of the organization, including communication and information. It was simple as focusing on the communication patterns of all employees that this led to a transformation in performance across the company.

Key points of communication

Face-to–face communication is the best type of communication. Your manager is the chief communicator. This means you need to be doing it frequently.

Effective communication begins with listening.

Talking in a group is also important for communication, problem solving and efficient information exchange.

You, as the manager, should create and leverage all communication means at your disposal in order to create a communication ecosystem that allows team members to support each other.

Communication Development

Personal Reflections

What about you? Have you ever felt part of a team, or organisation that communicated well with you? How did it feel?

Imagine a team with good communication skills. How did that feel?

Do you spend most your time on the phone?

How would you describe your ideal communication network?

Next Steps

Communication

Start with something you already know. Ask for feedback regarding how well you communicate.

Ask about the team's general sense of communication.

Evaluate the System

Find out the current information flow of your team members.

Think about the effectiveness of each tool and whether or not you will go further in using them.

Make sure to communicate often

There are many methods to improve communication skills, both in group and individual settings.

Read, study and listen. Practice, feedback, mentors and speaking groups.

Chapter 11: A Leaders Communication

Communication is essential for leadership. Great leaders openly communicate with their colleagues. This is often a two-route communication that encourages colleagues. It is not a progression of higher-lower demands from the leader. A leader who inspires the team and sets achievable goals, but challenges the team to reach their highest potential, is a successful leader. Leaders are often willing to go beyond their comfort zone in order to help others. Leaders encourage their staff to share ideas and make decisions when needed. Leaders have to have followers. It is common to recognize that leadership must involve interaction with others. The leader of a group will be someone, regardless of whether it's a small group of people working on a particular project, or a division within a large company. Leadership is usually formalized through the organization of a company. In these cases, the leaders have to be designated. Other times, the leader of a group can be removed as they work together.

Operative communication is the key to effective communication between the leader of the group and its members. Good leaders are skilled communicators. Sometimes however, great leaders' communication and interaction is misunderstood. Not everyone who just gives instructions is a great communicator. Leaders are able to openly communicate with their team. This is a two-way way of communicating that encourages members of the team to share their ideas. This communication is not about a strict top down flow of orders from the leader. Leaders are challenged with the responsibility of making sure that every member of the team has an understanding of his or her individual responsibilities and the goals of the group. The officeholder must also encourage participation. If you take a look at groups that aren't achieving their goals, you'll often see that there is something wrong with the group.

Be great at communicating. Communication is the most important skill. Leaders must be focused on improving their communication skills. It is important to communicate information both during normal work days and on challenging days. Many people know that communication is key to success. Poor communication is the number one problem in organizations. Communication problems can result from many things, including perceptual, attributional, interpersonal, top management, gender differences, physical separation, and organizational structure.

Our world has seen communication improve tremendously over the past decade thanks to technological advancements. It's easy for anyone to reach you in so many different ways. Mismanaging your communication with people can result in a loss of efficiency. There are some things you could do to help yourself avoid getting stressed. Bad communication can be costly and time-wasting in business. Research shows that 14% a week's work is wasted on poor communication. Intriguingly, strong communication can be a benefit to both associations and individuals. Work searchers will benefit from having strong relational skills, for example.

Encourage discussion and dialogue, instead of just talking

It is common to use the words dialog and discussion interchangeably to refer to verbal interaction between two individuals. There is however a significant difference. A discussion is characterized by an argumentative connotation. Participants in a conversation are most interested to advocate for their views and challenge other points. A conversation is similar to a discussion. Individuals involved in the conversation are more interested in convincing the other party to agree to their point of view. A mutual relationship is what the members seek in an exchange. Each member of the team should be given an opportunity to share their ideas and contribute to the team's goals. They will appreciate the opportunity to give feedback and make suggestions. This will help them to better understand the team's actions, and align their goals with the group's vision.

Communicate the Vision & Objectives in a logical and appropriate manner

As the leader of the team, it is your responsibility determine the final form or communicate instructions that have been given by higher management. Once you have done that, you should reach out to each member of your team for their input. Thank them for their contribution. If it was not the case, explain why. If your team members don't agree with the team's goals and objectives, then the team will not work at its best. If there is no chance for team members to contribute, such when orders are given from the upper management, then it is up to the leader to explain and defend the decision to the members. As the team leader, it is your responsibility to communicate the goals and plans to the team. You also need to make sure that everyone understands what they are expected. Leaders can use dialog to find out how their team members respond to the orders given to them and to allow them to voice their opinions.

Provide Regular Feedback

Be sure to remind the team about the group's purpose and goals. Charting the team's progress toward its goals is a great way to reinforce the end goal and keep the team appraised. A visual representation such as a scoreboard could make a significant difference. It is more difficult to show the objectives visually in ongoing teams like a work unit. However, it's important to quantify them as much and as accurately as possible. If necessary, feedback can be provided to the whole group. It can be used as motivation, encouragement, and also to correct course. Also, individual feedback sessions can be used to enhance the communication.

Regular check in conversations with each member of the team was a key part of the communication process for me. These conversations were separate from the regular performance reviews. Sometimes we might have a specific topic in mind, while other times we might just be asking a general question to start the conversation. You don't need to summon the other person, but you can go to their office regularly. (If you are talking about sensitive topics, you will need to make sure that there is a private space).

Be an active Listener

Communication is a process that involves listening. Effective leaders listen carefully to the speaker. Being attentive means paying attention and making eye contact. The other person needs to know that you are genuinely interested in her or his thoughts. Good leaders practice active listening. Active listening requires that the listener concentrate on the conversation, and respond appropriately to what is being said by the other party. You've likely been in conversations with people where you know that they are not listening to what you have to say. This situation is avoided with active listening. Active listeners are more attentive to the speaker and display verbal as well as non-verbal cues.

Non-verbal signs are maintaining eye contact and an attentive posture, such as leaning forward slightly, and responding with the appropriate facial expressions. Smiling in light moments or showing sympathy when needed are non-verbal signs. Active listeners do not distract themselves by fidgeting, looking at the clock or doing other distractions. These distracting nonverbal cues signify indifference as well as a lack respect. Participation in the conversation and verbal aspects of active listen include participation. You can ask relevant questions to show the speaker you are listening. These questions will help you to understand the speaker's message and provide clarity. Paraphrasing or repeating what a speaker said is a sign of attentiveness. This allows for dialogue to take place and increases the likelihood that the conversation will go further. You can also summarize what you have heard to help the speaker correct any mistakes.

Use Precise Communication

Use clear and confident language Get straight to the point. It is okay to give background information, but it is important to be specific about what you need. A concise, well-thought message communicates your message better than long, unfocused speeches. Avoid using acronyms, jargon, and other esoteric terms unless the listeners fully understand the meaning. To ensure the message is understood, check with the listener. Ask your listener what they understood. This will let the listener know if they received your message as intended.

Types and types of communication

Communication can be broken down into three basic types. Each type of communication has advantages and disadvantages.

Email

Thomas Jefferson summarized well-written guidelines in the following way: Avoid using two words when only one will do. To put it another way, two words can give you twice the effect. Writing more can make you sound more important. This is an old myth in business. Leaders who communicate clearly about their projects are more effective than those with too many words.

Stay current

If managing your email is a challenge, schedule some time to do administrative work. Emails must always be read. It is easy to become complacent or even fall behind if you don't check your email daily. It doesn't matter if you love it or not, email can be a vital part of the job.

Place an Out of Office

Keep an "Out of Office Note" in case you are absent from the office. The out of office message should contain the day and time you will be returning. If possible, provide an alternative or backup.

Send Once, Read Twice

It is vital that you go through your email at least two times before you send it. This will not only ensure you send out the right message but also protect you from appearing foolish.

When Sending Out Mass Emails

It is better to include all employees in your BCC field, when you are sending large numbers of emails. Employers will be prevented from sending replies via the BCC fields. This will decrease email clutter and will be appreciated by all who receive the email. It is important to be thorough when you send mass emails. You need to include contact information, locations, and other pertinent information. This will decrease the amount of questions or concerns that people might have.

Desk Phone

Your voicemail is set up

This may seem obvious, but this is something that I have come across many times. It can be easy to appear disorganized or seem uncaring if you don't have your voicemail setup.

Professional Voicemail Greetings

Professionalize your voicemail greeting. It is important that your voicemail message does not exceed 10 minutes in length.

Call Back

Do not procrastinate when you get voicemails. If you've received many calls, it is important to prioritize who gets the call back.

Set an Out of Office

It is important to ensure that there is an "Out of Office" message on both your desk telephone and your cell phone. It is not up to the caller to know what your schedule is. The out-of-office message should include your schedule and when you are expected back. If possible, provide an alternate contact or backup contact so they can reach you.

Cell Phone

Text messages

In order to send job requests and information, text messages have become more popular. I would try to avoid using text messaging as a primary means of communication. Sometimes it is necessary to ignore texts and phone calls. It may seem difficult to turn off the phone, but it is sometimes necessary. There are two things to consider: a text might be personal or commercial. It is difficult to concentrate on work if there are a lot text messages.

Place an Out of Office

It's a shame that I sound so blatantly insincere, but if you want people to reach you on your mobile phone for business, be sure to include an out-of office message if you are not at work, sick, vacation, or on holiday.

Instant Messaging

Sparely

Insta messaging is becoming a more common method of communication for companies. Instant messaging can be a great way of getting quick answers but it can also distract someone's attention. You must be careful with this.

Communicate Back

If you are not able to speak with someone right now, let them know so they can get back to you when they have more time. If you need to concentrate, either turn it off or set the "do no disturb" setting. There is a possibility that someone could reach out and disturb your concentration at any given moment.

Group Messaging

Use only for urgent messages

Sometimes, emailing urgent messages can prove too slow and may be overlooked by others. For urgent messages, group messaging may be a good tool.

You can set up a group for your team, as well as to communicate with leaders. This will allow for mass communication, which can be targeted to your target audience. It is crucial to ensure that you are following the rules. This communication type should be used only for urgent issues.

Keep one-on-1 conversations off the table

Group messages are for sharing information and working collaboratively with your team. If you have a message that needs multiple people or groups, this space is great. This space should not be used for personal conversations with colleagues. Even though it can be disruptive for individuals in meetings, team messaging is often very disruptive. For a direct conversation, you can call or message the individual. Your group will love you.

One-on-One Sessions for Employees

Monthly 1:1's

One on one meetings are a great method to make a connection with your employees. Every month, ensure you have completed your one on one with all of the employees.

This should be done quarterly for companies with more than 25 workers. If this is not done, it will take up a lot time that you could be focusing on other things.

Give them some time

While it is important to answer any questions that are asked by your leadership it is just as important to let the employee speak their mind. It is a good thing to be able to focus on the job and allow your employee to talk.

Public speaking

Public speaking is difficult for many people. Gloss Phobia is a fear of public speech and has been reported to affect 87% Americans. You are not alone. Most public speakers know this and understand the challenges of public speech.

Be prepared

How do you get into Carnegie Hall? Practice, Practice, Practice. When you have a presentation you need to make, spend some time working on it. Then, take it home to practice behind closed doors. It will help you become more comfortable with the content by allowing dry runs.

Know your Audience

You must remember who you are speaking to so that the message is tailored for them. You should not use jargon to present the information unless the audience knows the material. If you notice that the crowd is looking over at you, it is time to reconsider your approach.

Be You

If you are speaking in front a group, it is important not to try to imitate anyone but yourself. Some people may find you unauthentic and feel lost.

Tell A Story

It is important to be able connect with your audience. The presentation you give can be influenced by how personal it is.

Keep your Energy Level High

A speaker who is low in energy is the worst. They can absorb the energy and stop engaging the audience.

Paperwork

Despite physical paperwork becoming less common as technology advances, there are still many of them in the workplace.

Keep Some of Your Good Things.

Avoid the clutter. If a paper communication requires you to respond, immediately throw it out, file it, shred it.

Stay Organized

If you must keep a physical copy of your paperwork, be organized. You can put the document in a file called "Later" if you aren't available right away. Be sure to rank them by priority.

Find out what you can do

You don't necessarily need to keep a hard copy of the paperwork. Scan it using a copier, and then keep it organized on your computer.

Take out what you don't need

Do not keep any work documents. It will ensure that the communication is confidential and protect the environment.

Stay Current

Examine your documents at least once a quarter to ensure that they are current. If you aren't sure if the information is still necessary, scan it!

Chapter 12: Established Leadership Styles

This chapter will examine a list of classic and well-known leadership styles according US researcher Daniel Goleman. Goleman was able to identify and present the most common styles by conducting a study of more than 3000 high-ranking leaders. As his study has been considered an academic reference in the field, it was important that we start with these styles before looking at others.

Goleman realized that there were many styles to choose from when examining his findings. They adopt the style that best meets their immediate needs. All these styles can be part a leader's repertoire.

PACESETTING

Let's start with the pacesetting approach. This style is ideal for those times when you need to be fast and get things done. The pacesetting leader has high standards and high expectations. This style is best when quick results are essential. This style is most effective when the leader uses it.

Pay attention: Pacesetting can be too overwhelming for some team members, and it can also lower their morale.

Personal note - I have used this approach in leadership. It has produced results quickly and is highly effective. It is important that you and your team are on an unstoppable energy level. Otherwise, people can become tired. I prefer to be a pacesetting manager when necessary. Lead smart.

THE DEMOCRATIC

If the direction of an organization or company is unclear, the democratic method of leading can be used. This is when it's a good idea consult all your colleagues and staff before taking important decisions. This approach encourages consensus through participation rather than having one boss. This style could be something you should consider if it is important to be seen as a modern, inclusive leader. If it's done right, it's said to increase group commitment. This also allows you to draw on the expertise and knowledge of your staff.

Attention: It is not the most effective leadership style in times of crisis or when immediate decisions are required.

Personal note - I have chaired many meetings in this manner, which is greatly appreciated by employees who want a part of the business and to lead. However, it isn't the best to use when there is an urgent need.

THE COMMANDING/COERCIVE

The commanding method is a very old one. Sometimes it's called the military style. Despite the many downsides it has, it is still often used by leaders. It is believed to be efficient in situations of crisis or when it is necessary to make urgent decisions.

Attention: This is often a poor way to lead. It is not conducive to creativity and flexibility.

Personal note - I don't think I would like to be a leader using this commanding approach. However, it is something that I find valuable.

Imagine if there were an emergency of any type, like a fire, robbery, or other such thing, this could make it very useful for you to be able to command your troops as an effective military commander.

THE COACHING

Perhaps you are one among those leaders who loves helping your team achieve the goals they have set. If so, you're already using a coaching leadership style. This style is a great way to link individual goals with the goals for the entire organization. This is a classic one to one approach that focuses on staff members and how to make them more successful in the present and the future.

Attention: If there are lots of employees who are not open to changing and not interested in development, then coaching might not be the answer. This could lead to micro-management. It can backfire.

Personal note: If you work for a large corporation that has financial stability and allows for possible advancements and development, your coaching style can be a valuable tool for the company and you to build competent employees long term. Your coaching is appreciated by employees if they know that there will be more opportunities in the future for them and have the chance to get one. This idea can also be applied for smaller businesses. In fact, I have helped employees with this type of coaching in smaller businesses.

THE AFFILIATIVE

The strength in the affiliative leadership style lies in its ability to bring people together and create harmony within a group. This style works best when there is stress and when the team needs help to rebuild trust, or recovering from trauma. This approach values teamwork and sometimes creates a sense that employees are part of the company. This can be very useful.

This style is not recommended for use alone. If this style is too frequently used, it could lead to poor performance and unclear directions.

Personal note - I have had good experiences with this method so far, even though it is highly recommended to not use it exclusively. For many companies, the key to success is teamwork. It is difficult to achieve your goals when there is not harmony and a sense belonging within the group.

For example, football teams can be described as organizations that are working towards a common goal. The chances of reaching the finals are low if the players don't work in harmony and the group doesn't feel like they belong. My advice to you is to promote teamwork, and a sense belonging among your staff. This will make it easier to reach your goals.

THE VISIONARY

Visionary leaders can help organizations find a new direction, or simply to get them there. Visionary leaders are capable of mobilizing and moving people towards a common goal. The visionary will usually provide the end goal, but it is up to the employees how they get there. This makes employees feel more creative and innovative. They can freely experiment as long they work towards the same vision. So visionary leaders can often be a source of inspiration for entrepreneurs.

Attention: This may not be the best strategy if you have to lead a group of experts that are more knowledgeable than you about specific products, businesses, or how you can move forward.

Personal note - If you are in a position where others know more about you than you, this leadership style is still possible. Tell the group you don't know as much but you are here to help them reach their goals. Your job is to make long-lasting changes that benefit both the employees as well as the organization. You are the visionary. It is up to you to show everyone where you see yourself going. If you succeed, your followers will follow. Do your best at practicing this vision or speech at-home.

Chapter 13: Taking Risks

"There is risk and cost to action. But they are significantly less than the long term risks of passive inaction." JFK

Leaders are responsible for making decisions at all levels within a company. Every decision comes with risk. How do I assign this task to someone? How long should this take? What are the chances of it going wrong? Do I need to do this myself?

Leaders have to be able to answer these questions considering many factors. I was guilty, in my early days, of micromanagement. I wanted to do everything myself.

After completing my lengthy Army Officers Training, i reported directly to the unit, which was already activated to deploy that month. We completed daily exercises in the Ft. Bliss training phase. We learned how to respond to IEDs, clear buildings and sweep rooms, and what to do in case of an emergency. As a new lieutenant my first official assignment was as the headquarters leader. There were many administrative tasks required to ensure the unit was prepared for the next phase of going into war.

Every evening, the commander held a unit meeting. He reviewed everything each platoon needed to complete and, as the HQ Platoon, the majority of the work fell on me. We had to verify all training rosters were filed and ensure everyone was able to complete absentee voting ballots.

I completed most of the legwork for any assignment that was given me. I would take full responsibility and complete the task myself without the assistance of anyone else. I found myself in a rut and soon fell behind. I now see this as a blessing in disguise, because I was forced into enlisting the help of my soldiers. We kept up with everything once we started to delegate mundane administrative tasks.

I began to study the strengths and weaknesses in my soldiers. Some were skilled with computers, others were better communicators. I was able delegate certain responsibilities better to certain soldiers to increase our effectiveness. It was not perfect. I remember having a soldier drive to one of the ranges in order to validate paperwork from an instructor. He lost his way for four hours. We had to send an emergency search party. They found him driving aimlessly across the desert. I assumed he could map read. I was wrong.

Now we are in Iraq. Fast forward to a few more months. To meet the new mission requirements, we reorganized our unit into three combat units and one headquarters division. This experience taught me the importance and necessity to delegate tasks. Doing everything myself was impossible and shouldn't be an option. Only by delegating tasks, challenging your subordinates and taking chances to foster learning is the only way to truly be successful.

Leaders have to know when and how to limit risk. This is how to make employees leaders.

Who do you choose for task assignments?

There is no clear answer. Your competence plays a key role. You must first calculate all risks. Is this a routine, or not-essential task. Is the goal to be able to finish the task and avoid the business going bust? Or is it somewhere between?

Consider that you are in need of someone to drop off company mail daily. The person takes the mail every day, and returns it to you at the end. The contingency plan for this person is to make sure it gets done on the next day. It's easy enough.

This is the perfect opportunity for you to assign an additional task to a younger, less-experienced and/or more challenging employee. You could also give this opportunity to your less experienced employee to increase his sense of responsibility. Managers are often unaware of the seriousness with which employees take on their responsibilities. Managers can take on too much responsibility and deny employees their ability to handle it.

These employees then become disengaged, lose their motivation and adopt a who gives two halves philosophy. Management becomes a disciplinarian and resorts to the threat or termination to motivate employees. What a system!

It's how most businesses are managed, and that starts with leadership. This is where the power and gift of delegation can really make a difference. By delegating a simple task but important, even the lowest performers can contribute all they can.

Another example is when you have a legal form that must be signed by your most important client. If that signature does not make it to the office within the time frame, the contract will be cancelled. Failure to do so could cause financial damage for the company and its most valuable client. Assuming this is impossible to complete, this seems like a job for one of your most competent employees who understands the situation and has been reliable.

Sometimes, legal signatures and mail drop-offs are more complicated than they seem. There are usually many moving parts and more factors that you need to consider. Here is where you must calculate the risks. Below are some questions you should ask before delegating tasks.

The Seven Delegation Risk Questions

How long should I spend analyzing the details, forming a plan and making a decision before taking a final call?

What happens if this task is not completed successfully?

What could happen to make this task a complete failure?

What are your contingency plans in the event of a catastrophic failure? What is the cost to you and your staff in terms both time and money?

This is a task that I should be able to manage myself.

Is it too much for my employee?

Is it necessary for my employee to be challenged, and is he ready and able?

You can't guarantee success when delegating. And it takes time and practice to be able to accurately calculate risks. By answering these questions, you will be able better to gauge who should complete a task. Sometimes it is OK to make mistakes.

Every once in awhile, new agents come to our agency. I now understand the learning curve and can expect to make mistakes. I'm open to the most common mistakes as it gives me an opportunity for reflection on their actions, the reasons they made it and the next steps. It doesn't matter if they make the same mistake again, the experience will be a valuable learning opportunity.

Situation: My new role is that of Executive Officer (XO). My primary role is ensuring the unit's mission readiness, conducting training, and providing guidance and direction to the other lieutenants.

As the Commander's Right-hand Man, I was responsible for all the lieutenants of our unit. Every few months, a fresh lieutenant would become available. I saw the anxiety and discomfort in delegating authority with every new lieutenant. They weren't afraid of delegating but were concerned about the results.

They weren't sure things would get done and started micromanaging. They would continually look at their subordinates to make sure they were following the rules. This was an expression of their anxiety and stress. They would sometimes take over and do everything all by themselves.

That's annoying for subordinates, but it also indicates a lack in trust, faith, confidence. If the behavior goes on for too long, soldiers' attitude and performance will suffer. While I would let them go through the phase, I would also intervene and help them see that what they were doing in micromanagement could have long-lasting effects that could affect our unit's combat readiness.

When I first entered civilian life, I was just like everyone else. One thing I noticed was very significant that is still true to this day. Common leadership mistakes are made whenever someone moves from an employment position to a management one. As we explained earlier, micromanaging employees by a new manager is common. Insecurity and feelings of uneasiness can develop and often last until the new boss settles in to her new role. Sometimes it can take weeks.

This is why mistakes are inevitable. Most of them will be simple and predictable. Delegating responsibility is always a risk. Consider the seven questions you have been asked and the answers that you will get. Next, think about the steps. Simpler tasks like dropping off mail will still require the same answers as more complex ones. These questions will help you to identify the best person for the job.

Important note: Everyone learns from mistakes. Failure to do so can lead to a lost opportunity, which will increase the chance of it happening again.

You will be amazed at how productive you organization can become when you learn to delegate. You can sit back and enjoy all the details. You don't have to get in the way of delegating. Secondary responsibilities will include supporting your employees as necessary. You can provide support for your employees in many ways, including extra office supplies, increased work space, software or hardware that is better, as well as an assistant. The leader is responsible for ensuring that highly productive employees have the support they need in order to perform their jobs.

What if I don't really know my staff?

This is an important concern. I've already mentioned that the first period as a leader is vulnerable, because you don't get to know your staff very well. Delegating tasks is still necessary. Do not forget to pay particular attention when delegating tasks. Did the employee rush the task or produce sloppy work? They took much longer than they needed, but they still got great results. Did the employee come up with a ridiculously inefficient way of completing the task but still achieve satisfactory results? Did the employee take more time than necessary, yet still produce sloppy results. Does the worker seem like his work is not up to par? Do you think the employee was too quick but did a great work? Any observation is good.

These questions give you an indication of the type and attitude of the employee that you are dealing. However, if you see an employee who is slow to respond and does not do a good job, it doesn't necessarily indicate that he is a bad worker. It is more likely that he only needs good leadership to bring him up-to-speed.

I had the pleasure of meeting a soldier serving in Iraq, who was on desk duties due to a temporary medical condition. I asked him to walk around the compound, find out how many trailers there were and their current state. It was easy. He returned within 10 seconds to our headquarters saying, "We've got two of them, and they work well." I knew there would be at least five in the compound so they had to be located and inspected. He was indicating that there were many issues that needed fixing. After I spoke with him about my concerns, it became clear that he was not just discouraged at being stuck on base but capable of so much more. He did not need to be considered a bad subordinate.

Just by watching an employee perform a task, you can learn a lot more about them. Chapter 9 will detail additional steps that you can take to learn more about your staff.

Make sure you are ready for any mistakes

There will always be mistakes when you take risks. If they don't, you aren't challenging anybody. Which is a far more grave evil. These mistakes will be avoided if you carefully answer the Six Risk Calculation Question below.

The mistake is your fault. I don't know how often I've seen Army Officers or Agency Supervisors blame a subordinate because of a mistake. It's like forcing someone into a fire to save you. Every decent person in the upper management will respect your ability to accept responsibility. However, if you are disappointed in an employee, they may have their own problems. You can take responsibility for the situation and move on.

Have a full discussion about the nature and consequences of the error. Discuss the matter with your employees. Find out what went wrong, what was done differently, and ensure everyone is fully informed. This should be an opportunity to share constructive feedback. Placing blame is counterproductive. Finding future solutions is the goal. It is important to keep control of meetings because they are susceptible to getting off track.

Be open to suggestions and corrections. Sometimes people can have great ideas even though a meeting is over. Keep in mind that everyone should bring up an idea if it occurs. It may be what you need for the next level, or to solve the problem that led to the initial mistake.

The Difficult Decisions

Making a difference as a leader requires a lot of hard work, but it is rewarding. Leadership can be difficult when there are many decisions to be made and information is scarce. When you're faced with a decision, there is no other option than to take a calculated risk.

Lt. Lox from the 101st Airborne division was a colleague of mine and faced such a decision. His platoon drove through a valley while on a reconnaissance trip to Afghanistan. Taliban fighters were known as being able to access the valley. The Taliban used the valley as a base. His platoon got ambushed mid-way through. They were able, however, to break contact and push to the opposite end of the valley. There was some vehicle damage but no injuries. His unit quickly regrouped, and Lieutenant Lox was confronted with a difficult choice. His platoon could go back to base via an alternate route. However, that would mean that the mission would take significantly longer. It was also unclear if all of his vehicles would make it back due to damage. This further complicated the problem. Or he could go the fastest route through the valley and barrel through it, returning to base in less time than the alternative route. The risk of another, worse ambush is there. He was pressured to make the right decision because his senior sergeants were divided. It would only create more problems if they kept their current positions.

Risk was a part of every decision. Your leadership role will require you to make decisions that could have unintended consequences. Your staff will look at you for direction when there is pressure. Training is essential. Training equips people for all situations. If you do not prepare your team for emergencies, it will become a problem.

In the end, Lt. Lox decided to take the fastest route back to the base and go through the valley. His logic was that IEDs would not be placed by the Taliban, which was the most hazardous possibility. He believed that running into small arms fire in the same area was the best route. He was right. They actually dispersed the Taliban before they got through and they did not take any fire. It's a good thing, because one of them barely made it back home to base.

Chapter 14: Task-Oriented Leadership

Every business has people working on it. Leaders can either concentrate on the work that is being completed or the people who complete it, or both. As their name suggests, task-oriented leaders pay more attention to the work they are doing. They are extremely goal-focused, and they work efficiently to attain predetermined goals.

This type leadership cares less about the performance of the teams and individuals performing the work. The work must be completed on time and to the expected standard. Task-orientated leaders will determine the roles in a team, split the work up between them, establish processes, procedures and monitor progress. Everything and everyone is focused on achieving the task.

Most businesses succeed or fail due to their ability and willingness to create and deliver products and/or services. A business' success depends on the creation and delivery of high-quality products. A task-oriented leader will have a clear, direct approach to getting things done for the betterment of the business. Products have to be made, and employees are required to make them. They must also deliver the services.

There is little attention paid to the values, attitudes, and feelings of staff. They are there for a job, and the task-oriented leader should maximize their productivity. This leadership style is all about task cohesion. That is, the staff are motivated to succeed by achieving goals and objectives. It is a positive thing for staff to work together toward achieving a common goal. This will make them feel more satisfied and motivate them to do more.

Principal Strengths

This style of leadership has the obvious advantage that it meets deadlines and ensures tasks are completed. It can be extremely useful for industries that have to meet stringent deadlines while still maintaining high quality standards. Multiple assembly-line manufacturing and media publications are examples of this. You must complete work within a given time and at a particular standard. There is limited room for error and delays. This role may suit someone who is a task-oriented leader.

The key strength of task-oriented leadership lies in their ability to delegate effectively and to know how to prioritise and split work so that they can get things done. They will have a deep understanding of what resources are needed to complete the task. This can make them highly efficient in their planning as well as implementation. This can increase productivity and help to save money within the company.

Businesses are measured largely on their productivity. If these levels rise, the task-oriented leader will be able to provide growth and survival for his business and job security for his staff. These positive outcomes offer an indirect benefit to employees, even though they are not intended to meet their immediate needs.

Key Criticisms

The main problem with task-orientated leaders is that they can neglect the welfare and happiness their staff. If the leader is too focused on the task, it can lead to the leader not addressing key issues within the team. In order to make the team feel valued and appreciated, it is important to not only focus on the task at hand but also to pay attention to personal needs. Although productivity should be a priority, task-oriented leaders can in fact reduce productivity indirectly. Employees who feel undervalued and not appreciated are less likely to be motivated and achieve their potential.

This task-oriented leadership doesn't allow staff to be creative, inventive, or spontaneous in the work they do. Instead, they are expected and required to follow orders. Each task is a mini-task that they must complete. There is not much room for creativity or adaptability. This style of leadership can result in staff losing enthusiasm, motivation, and the ability to do more than they are expected. The lack of opportunities to experiment with new ideas can limit staff's ability to advance into more complex jobs. This environment restricts staff development opportunities because it is harder to progress and train.

If staff feel disengaged and unmotivated, they will not stay in their jobs for long. High productivity will not translate into high turnover, which will cause additional time to train and recruit new staff. This can have an adverse effect on the team, as staff turnover can lead to disruptions in key processes.

There is a demand for task-oriented leaders in every industry. Without them, it would be difficult for many tasks to get completed. The leader can neglect to address the needs or the interests of the staff if they only push them to complete their tasks. This can lead both to poor staff welfare and high levels of demotivation.

Employees that feel undervalued and unappreciated will lose their motivation to work which in turn will lead to lower productivity, something task-oriented leaders seek to address. This is why task-oriented leadership needs to be used together with other styles of leadership to ensure staff feel valued, appreciated, and motivated to work.

We all have to meet deadlines. And leaders must make sure that other people do the same. Of course, we may subconsciously lead in this way due to pressures from others. But it is important for us to maintain a balance between this style of leadership and one that also considers the needs of our staff. This final thought brings us nicely onto the next chapter where we will be exploring relationship-orientated leadership.

Relationship-Orientated Leadership

The previous chapter started by suggesting that leaders have two options: they can concentrate on the work being accomplished or the people performing it, and either one or both. In direct contrast to task-orientated leaders, relationship-orientated leaders are primarily focused on the people who perform the work. They want to support, motivate, and develop people and teams. They want to have meaningful relationships that are mutually beneficial and use this connection to improve staff performance.

Advanced levels of emotional intelligence are required for effective relationship-orientated leadership. This allows them the ability to empathise well with their staff, and see things through their eyes. Relationship-orientated leaders encourage effective teamwork and collaboration through enhanced relationships that exist between team members. Understanding the needs and requirements of each individual person is vital if relationship-orientated leadership is to be effective.

Relationship-orientated leaders are very personable, their 'door is always open' and they have a genuine interest in the wellbeing of their staff. They support and look after their employees in a way they can perform at their best.

Social cohesion in the team can foster relationships. If the leader ensures that there is a strong social cohesion within the team, he or she can keep staff inspired and motivated to work. This leadership style fosters collaboration within the group and encourages everyone to want each other's success and development.

Principal Strengths

By focusing on the emotional needs of the staff, relationship-orientated leaders are able to ensure they have a positive and motivated workforce. Staff will feel valued and appreciated by their leaders and be more excited about work. A highly motivated team will encourage greater productivity, even though it is often not necessary to direct attention to task completion.

With a supportive team of staff, personal conflict, dissatisfaction, boredom and other issues will be reduced, which results in a happy and productive work environment. Personal issues will not hinder staff's ability to work efficiently and at a better standard. Staff performance is often affected by interpersonal and social issues. It is possible to reduce these issues by making sure they are happy, excited, and supported at work.

Staff may also be more willing to take risks and challenge key operations, creating new and creative work. Because staff know the leader is there to support them in failure, they will feel comfortable taking risks. This is important for the development of staff and improving organisational performance.

Key Criticisms

A major criticism of relationship-orientated leadership is that with a major focus on the relationships between staff the actual task being performed can sometimes be overlooked. Staff may not want to be worked too hard, too frequently, or in an environment they do not like. This can increase the likelihood of them failing. You may need to be more focused on the task when there are strict deadlines and you have to work hard.

Another problem is that some employees might see the leader as a person-focused leader. Staff might take liberties when they see the leader accommodating all their needs. Like a child trying to get along with his teacher or parent, staff may push the limits to see how much they can accomplish. A bond between an employee and a leader is more likely because there will be a high level of mutual understanding. But this is not something that happens instantly. Leaders must also be aware of employee attempts to push the boundaries.

While the encouragement of risk taking is a key strength of relationship-orientated leadership it can also be considered a criticism. While risk-taking is crucial for the progress of an organisation, it needs to be balanced with the need to manage risk. It is possible to make irreversible and costly mistakes if you take too much risk.

Leaders have to be relationship-focused; after all, leadership is all about inspiring and motivating people to take action. They will not succeed if they don't get the needs, desires, and abilities of their employees. This being said, it's important that leaders keep their eyes on what they are doing. In order to satisfy the ever-growing demands of staff members, a leader may lose sight of the task. This could impact the long-term performance.

You must find the right balance between staff and task needs. The key is to ensure the support provided is tied directly to the completion the task. This will empower staff and help them do the best job possible. We began the chapters by saying that leaders have the option of focusing their attention either on the work itself or on the people who are doing it. The obvious answer is either.

Chapter 15: Continue To Expand Your Skills

True managers never stop learning.

They are always looking to expand their knowledge and skills.

They cannot sit still. They love to read, train, take refresher classes, and learn how to improve their productivity.

Even when the company has been doing well they have the ability to see beyond the current situation and to assume any future challenges. However, they also keep their eyes open for opportunities that could jeopardize the company's success.

The world is continually changing, and it is imperative to always be evolving in order to keep up the competition. Keeping the status-quo is impossible today.

Never base critical decisions on the organizational structure of a company. Instead adapt it to the market.

This structure must be flexible so that it can adapt to changes.

Consider identifying a mentor in your own life. Our lives are made up of people we have encountered along the way. We are never satisfied with our current state of learning. At any age, we can always find someone who can give us a lesson.

Never ever doubt that you are capable.

Even if your position is at the top, you still need to set an example.

Always ask yourself the following question: "Who are my mentors right now?" If you don't find the answer to your question, run for cover as quickly as possible.

Everyone needs someone to look up to in order to grow and improve.

The training of your staff is as important as the training you receive as a team leader.

Companies will only succeed if they have great employees. If you do not invest in training, employees will stop using their brains fully and lose motivation.

A company with no future will decide to cut back on its training budget. It will be too late once they realize.

Be confident in your ability to surround yourself and others with competent people.

" A lot of people do whatever is necessary

Get the next promotion.

All I ever wanted was to be in the Navy

The command of a ship.

I didn't mind if I was ever promoted again.

This attitude enabled me to be successful.

It is better to be focused on results than doing

What are the 'right things' for me in my career?

It was my friends that I met along the journey.

These were the results that made sure

My next promotion

(Michael Abrashoff)

The secret to success is in this sentence: "it was my people that created my results that ensured that my next job promotion."

It's a significant difference. While managers might not always value this aspect, some companies may not always be able support it. There is no other explanation.

An honest manager will understand this. A leader who is self-respecting will not think about his personal gain and limit the growth potential of his staff will lose the ability to lead.

It's no surprise that the world is filled with managers who need to surround them with incompetent staff to confirm their talents and abilities.

They will need shameless 'yesmen' to lick their chops beside them, who will always pander for their good fortunes.

These are not leaders. Managing resources this way will only stunt the creativity and innovation of the staff, who will simply follow the orders of their manager.

Another thing that a leader must avoid is seeing reality from only his point of view. Our collaborators are constantly providing us with new stimuli or information, often without our conscious awareness. It's up for us to collect them, analyze and decide which ones will be most helpful to our cause.

To help us attain that goal we ask the simple question, "If you adopted this solution would it benefit my team and our process of production?"

It's hard for us to accept the possibility that a method that we consider working well might need to be changed or updated. There are often many different ways to address a problem. Some may be easier, more cost-effective, or better for our relationships with colleagues.

"Learn and listen to remember."

Silence often leads to silence

These same effects can be achieved with knowledge.

Be proud of your accomplishments, however

ask questions."

(Jerry Manas)

Asking questions is not a sign to be weak or insecure but rather a sign for maturity and intelligence. Asking questions will be more productive than receiving directives and issuing orders. Listening to different points of view is the only way forward.

Your partner should feel free to ask open-ended questions. They should feel free to express themselves without fear.

It's better to find out what is going wrong within your team and to tell your boss than to keep your head down when your co-workers are saying that it is wrong or that there is another way.

"I don't want any Yesmen around my house.

I want everyone telling me

The truth, even though

It cost him his job."

(Samuel Goldwyn)

There are many managers who think they are great leaders and don't realize that their employees do not value them. It is simply because they have never listened.

Do not stop the flow of innovative ideas.

Leaders favor operational people who are capable of solving problems by simply doing the job according to the established procedures. The idea of proposing new solutions is seen as a waste and discourages employees from suggesting innovative ideas.

Brain writing, which is replacing brainstorming, can help. You could instead of asking your thoughts to be shared, ask for your solution in writing at the start of a meeting.

A colleague can take the paper and read it aloud to you. You can pass the paper to a colleague next to you who will read the proposal aloud. This way, everyone will have their say.

Do it several times and you'll be amazed at how many new ideas can spark interesting discussions.

"Too many people are leaders when they get too many."

I'm in the throes a self-congratulation.

No longer will I hear any criticism of the

Their opinions... this is where the good stuff happens

Ideas are stifled, and people stop listening.

Carry them on, and support them."

(Larry Bossidy)

You should treasure criticism, even if it is constructive.

Conclusion

The idea of being a leader is very different to being a boss is something we still believe in. You may have heard that leaders do what is right, while managers do the right. This distinction can be very delicate as many leaders also work as managers. Perhaps the main difference is that leaders can create and communicate a compelling vision that is often tied to change. Managers might tend to be more involved with maintaining the status, however.

Not being raised, but becoming a better leader. You can be a good leader if your heart is open to it. A leader who is a good learner, prepares, and experiences often has a high success rate.

There are certain things that you need to know to help your employees achieve greater teamwork. These skills are not easy to acquire, but they are possible through continual study and continuous hard work. Good leaders study constantly to improve their leadership skills.

The truth is that it's impossible to lead in all circumstances. This is why flexibility and adaptability are important characteristics for leaders who can handle changing circumstances. People are attracted to employers who can motivate, excite and build respect.

Leaders are those who have credibility and inspire others to follow them. This definition shows that leadership skills can be applied to all situations in which you are required or expected to exercise leadership, at home, in professional settings, and in social situations.

Once you're able to see it, people will naturally admire you as leader. There are many ways you can be a leader.

you can get elected,

You can choose to be included

It is possible.

You can bring down other people and become a great leader. Or, people will raise you up because they see you're able either to see something or you're able achieve something they don't know how to do.

www.ingramcontent.com/pod-product-compliance
Lightning Source LLC
Chambersburg PA
CBHW050405120526
44590CB00015B/1834